Falling Behind or Moving Up? The Intergenerational Progress of Mexican Americans

• • •

Jeffrey Grogger
Stephen J. Trejo

2002

PUBLIC POLICY INSTITUTE OF CALIFORNIA

Library of Congress Cataloging-in-Publication Data
Grogger, Jeffrey, 1959–
    Falling behind or moving up? : the intergenerational progress of
Mexican Americans / Jeffrey Grogger, Stephen J. Trejo.
        p. cm.
    Includes bibliographical references.
    ISBN 1-58213-049-3
    1. Mexican Americans—Economic conditions. 2. Mexican
Americans—Social conditions. 3. Mexican American families—
Economic conditions. 4. Mexican American families—Social
conditions. 5. Intergenerational relations—Economic aspects—
United States. 6. Mexican Americans—Statistics. 7. United
States—Economic conditions—2001- 8. United States—Social
conditions—1980- I. Trejo, Stephen J., 1959– II. Title.

E184.M5 G79 2002
305.868'72073—dc21   2002067929

Foreword

The power of intergenerational progress is a central tenet of the American Dream: Each generation stands on the shoulders of the preceding one, and improvement in health, income, and well-being is assured through education and hard work. For immigrants, intergenerational improvement is taken for granted—whether European immigrants at the turn of the twentieth century or Latino and Asian immigrants at the turn of the twenty-first century. With California's population growing by 10 million residents in the past twenty years, and immigrants accounting for well over half of that growth, it has never been more important that the American Dream not lose its luster. Yet we face the prospect that future generations of Californians may not experience the rapid progress that earlier generations took for granted.

Building on earlier studies of Mexican Americans in California, Jeffrey Grogger and Stephen Trejo conclude that "intergenerational progress for Mexican Americans appears to stall after the second generation, with only modest improvement in educational attainment and no wage growth observed between the second and third generations." This is an important finding, and it needs further study to determine the precise nature and causes of the problem.

The authors analyze Mexican immigrants and U.S.-born Mexican Americans separately (as others should do when looking at California's demographic trends), and they find that educational improvement is crucial to the earnings progress of all Mexican Americans because the schooling levels of people of Mexican descent lag behind those of almost all other groups in America.

There is no doubt that California faces a significant challenge in the coming decades. The burden will fall squarely on the shoulders of the K–12 education system to make sure that the schools, teachers, and curriculum are there to keep the American Dream alive for Mexican Americans, both immigrants and native born. And the ongoing public debate over the merits of immigration will rely heavily on a clear understanding of how each new wave of arrivals is doing in achieving the dream.

Calculating the costs and benefits of immigration to California and the nation has become a regular exercise for special committees, commissions, and research centers and institutes. If intergenerational improvement in education, jobs, and earnings does not occur at a predictably high rate, the political pressure to more carefully monitor immigration will surely intensify. The findings in this report are a new and important contribution for those making the calculations, because Grogger and Trejo focus exclusively on Mexican Americans. Their initial findings do not present an especially hopeful portrait.

The findings also raise the prospect that widening income disparity in California will continue well into the future and perhaps will even generate a further widening of the gap between the top and bottom levels of the state's income distribution. PPIC research fellow Deborah Reed concluded in her most recent analysis of income disparity in the state that the "growing overrepresentation of immigrants in the bottom categories [of wages] has contributed strongly to rising income inequality in California." While many Mexican American immigrants start out at the bottom of the wage scale, it is neither desirable nor expected that they will languish there for two more generations. Grogger and Trejo suggest that this prospect is a real possibility for some, and that public policy must be finely tuned to offset this possibility.

Numerous studies have focused on the rate and degree to which current waves of immigrants are integrated into the political economy of America. One review, carried out by the National Research Council in a report entitled *The New Americans: Economic, Demographic, and Fiscal Effects of Immigration,* concludes that the integration of new immigrants and subsequent generations is highly correlated with education and the wage gains that are associated with returns to skill. Again, all roads lead to education—whether the roads relate to higher earnings, reduced income disparity, or participation in civic life.

This work by Grogger and Trejo is a substantial contribution to our understanding of the intergenerational progress of Mexican Americans and the issues that are raised by the prospect that, for some families, the

American Dream might be a bridge too far. There is much to be learned from future work on this subject, and Grogger and Trejo have already focused the spotlight on a key topic for the economic, social, and political future of California: What are the prospects for Mexican Americans and what role will public policy play in keeping the California version of the American Dream alive? The authors' findings suggest that the challenge is great and that there is every good reason to focus public attention on the resources that are needed to educate current and future generations of Mexican Americans.

David W. Lyon
President and CEO
Public Policy Institute of California

Summary

Mexican immigrants and their descendants constitute a sizable and rapidly growing segment of the U.S. population. This is particularly true in California, where over 20 percent of the population is of Mexican descent.

Mexican Americans are also one of the most economically disadvantaged groups in the United States, with an average household income that is more than 40 percent below the comparable average for non-Hispanic whites.[1] Disagreement persists over the prospects for Mexican Americans joining the economic mainstream of American society. Chavez (1991) claims that the large influx of recent immigrants from Mexico creates a deceptively pessimistic picture of Mexican-origin workers in the U.S. labor market, and that U.S.-born, English-speaking Mexican Americans have enjoyed rapid progress over the last couple of decades and are approaching the labor market status of non-Hispanic whites. According to Chavez, Mexican Americans are climbing the economic ladder across generations in the same way as earlier waves of white immigrants from Europe. In contrast, Chapa (1990) sees little evidence that Mexican Americans are making steady progress toward economic parity with non-Hispanic whites, and he worries about the emergence of a Chicano underclass with many of the same problems faced by inner-city blacks.

To better understand the current and future economic prospects of Mexican Americans, we analyze the intergenerational progress of Mexican-origin workers in the California and U.S. labor markets. In the first part of our report, we use recent data from the Current Population Survey (CPS) to compare the educational attainment and hourly earnings

---

[1]In this report, we refer to people of Mexican descent living in the United States as Mexican Americans. We distinguish between Mexican immigrants and U.S.-born Mexican Americans only when the distinction is germane to the discussion.

of whites, blacks, and three generations of Mexican Americans (with the first generation consisting of Mexican immigrants, the second generation including the U.S.-born children of Mexican immigrants, and the third generation referring to their grandchildren and later descendants). We find that people of Mexican descent acquire much less schooling than other groups in the United States, and that this educational deficit is the main reason for the relatively low earnings of Mexican-origin workers. Thus, the fundamental economic problem confronting Mexican Americans is insufficient schooling. In the second part of our report, we try to learn more about this important problem. We use data from the National Education Longitudinal Study (NELS) to examine in detail the determinants of racial and ethnic differences in a key educational outcome: high school graduation.[2]

Education and Wage Patterns

The main empirical findings of the first part of our report are as follows:

1. Mexican Americans experience dramatic gains in education and earnings between the first and second generations. On average, U.S.-born Mexican Americans have three and a half years more schooling and at least 30 percent higher wages than do Mexican immigrants.

2. Intergenerational progress for Mexican Americans appears to stall after the second generation, with only modest improvement in educational attainment and no wage growth observed between the second and third generations. A possible reason is that the intergenerational transmission of education is much weaker among Mexican Americans than among other groups. As a result, the dramatic gains between immigrants and their children do not translate into additional gains for subsequent generations.

3. Substantial education and wage deficits persist between U.S.-born Mexican Americans and other Americans. Among the

---

[2]Both the CPS and NELS surveys include data from undocumented immigrants, although neither survey identifies them separately.

third generation, for example, Mexican Americans average a year and a half less schooling and about 25 percent lower wages than non-Hispanic whites.

4. The educational disadvantage of Mexican-origin workers is the principal reason why they earn less than other U.S. workers. Among men and women born in the United States, racial/ethnic differences in observable indicators of skill—in this case, age and years of schooling—explain from one-half to three-quarters of the wage gaps between Mexican and white workers, with schooling accounting for most of the difference.[3] By contrast, observable skill differences account for only about one-third of black-white wage gaps.

5. The labor market payoff to acquiring a high school diploma through an equivalency exam such as the GED, rather than through the usual coursework, is substantially higher for Mexican immigrants than for U.S.-born workers of any race/ethnicity.

Determinants of High School Graduation

Immigration plays a tremendous role in the white-Mexican graduation gap, even among young cohorts of workers. Youths who immigrate to the United States between the ages of 15 and 21 have high school completion rates of only 28 percent, in contrast to the 87 percent completion rate of U.S.-born whites and the 78 percent completion rate of U.S.-born blacks. Mexican youths who arrive in the United States between the ages of 5 and 15 do only a bit better, eventually completing high school at a rate of only 40 percent.

Children who arrive before age 5 do much better; about 78 percent eventually complete high school. Indeed their graduation rates are similar to those of both U.S.-born students of Mexican heritage and blacks. Within their age cohort, these U.S.-born and "near-native" students of Mexican heritage compose about 65 percent of all persons of

---

[3]Henceforward, the term "white" refers to those who are white and not Hispanic.

Mexican heritage in the United States. We analyze a number of factors to understand why this group graduates at lower rates than whites.

Consistent with prior findings on minority-white attainment differentials, we find that family income plays an important role, explaining as much as 75 percent of the white-Mexican graduation gap. However, independent of income, maternal education plays a very small role, despite the fact that the parents of Mexican American students have very low education levels. The reason is that, for this group, maternal education has little independent effect on students' graduation prospects. This finding helps resolve the heretofore puzzling observation that the educational progress of Mexican Americans seems to stall between the second and third generations. If the intergenerational transmission of education were as strong among Mexican Americans as among other groups, then the dramatic gains in education between immigrants and their children would translate into further progress among later generations. Since the transmission mechanism for Mexican Americans is so weak, educational progress largely stops with the children of immigrants. These results contrast to those for blacks, for whom maternal education strongly predicts graduation and explains an important fraction of the black-white graduation gap, even controlling for family income.

We also consider the role of a number of variables that may reflect the results of parents' actions to influence the educational environment facing their children. Familial communication, social capital, and after-school care arrangements prove helpful both in predicting graduation and in explaining the family income effect for students of Mexican heritage. Some literacy-related measures such as library use and the possession of reading and reference materials are less important for Mexican American students than they are for whites and blacks, however. There is some indirect evidence that part of the family income effect for Mexican American families operates through the schools that their children attend.

In general, our results point to the importance of family background for explaining graduation rates and graduation rate differentials. We identify some of the factors that underlie the link between parental education, family income, and children's educational success. The results leave many further questions, however, such as why certain family characteristics matter more for some racial/ethnic groups than for others. Although it is fairly clear that family characteristics bear importantly on children's educational success, more work is needed to better understand why.

Conclusions and Implications

An important implication of our findings is that Mexican immigrants and U.S.-born Mexican Americans are distinct groups with very different skills and labor market opportunities. Therefore, analyses that do not distinguish between these groups can give a misleading impression of Mexican economic progress in the United States. Although perhaps an obvious point, and not a new one, it bears repeating because many media and policy discussions of Mexican Americans continue to lump together immigrants and U.S. natives. Given the strikingly low education and wages of Mexican immigrants, aggregation masks the substantial intergenerational gains that occur. The experiences of second- and third-generation Mexican Americans reveal the long-term economic prospects of the Mexican-origin population, and these prospects are considerably brighter than what is suggested by statistics that do not distinguish between foreign-born immigrants and U.S.-born Mexican Americans.

Our findings also indicate that increasing educational attainment is the key to improving the economic status of Mexican Americans. That more and better schooling would help any group has the ring of a truism, especially in times of rising demand for skilled workers. But educational improvements are crucial to the earnings progress of Mexican Americans to a much larger extent than for blacks and other disadvantaged groups, because their schooling levels lag behind those of almost all other groups in America. Moreover, the economic payoff to educational investments is about as high for U.S.-born Mexican Americans as for other U.S. natives, especially in California. Finding a way to somehow eliminate the educational disadvantage of Mexican Americans would go a long way toward bringing this group into the economic mainstream. For Mexican immigrants who arrive as teenagers or adults, the GED is a promising avenue for increasing education and ultimate earnings. The GED seems to provide a mechanism through which immigrants can certify their educational qualifications for U.S. employers who do not know how to evaluate credentials earned in Mexico or other foreign countries.

Contents

Tables

Acknowledgments

This report has benefited from advice and comments by Melissa Binder, Gary Bjork, Hans Johnson, Meredith Phillips, Deborah Reed, Cordelia Reimers, and Belinda Reyes. We are grateful for their help and also for the outstanding research assistance of Duncan MacRae. Nevertheless, the authors are solely responsible for the content of this report.

1. Introduction

Mexican immigrants and their descendants constitute a sizable and rapidly growing segment of the U.S. population. This is particularly true in California, where over 20 percent of the population is Mexican American.[1] Mexican Americans are also one of the most economically disadvantaged groups in the United States, with an average household income that is more than 40 percent below the comparable average for non-Hispanic whites.[2]

Disagreement persists over the prospects for Mexican Americans joining the economic mainstream of American society. Chavez (1991) claims that the large influx of recent immigrants from Mexico creates a deceptively pessimistic picture of Mexican-origin workers in the U.S. labor market and that U.S.-born, English-speaking Mexican Americans have enjoyed rapid progress over the last couple of decades and are approaching the labor market status of non-Hispanic whites. According to Chavez, Mexican Americans are climbing the economic ladder across generations in the same way as earlier waves of white immigrants from Europe. In contrast, Chapa (1990) sees little evidence that Mexican Americans are making steady progress toward economic parity with non-Hispanic whites, and he worries about the emergence of a Chicano underclass with many of the same problems faced by inner-city blacks.

Existing research provides some empirical support for each side of this debate. On the one hand, as stressed by Chavez (1991), dramatic improvements in human capital and earnings take place between Mexican immigrants and the U.S.-born children of immigrants (Smith, 1991). On the other hand, intergenerational progress appears to stall

---

[1]In this report, we refer to people of Mexican descent living in the United States as Mexican Americans. We distinguish between Mexican immigrants and U.S.-born Mexican Americans only when the distinction is germane to the discussion.

[2]This income comparison is based on calculations from March 1996–1999 Current Population Survey (CPS) data that are reported in Figures 2 and 3 of Bean et al. (2001).

after the second generation (Trejo, 1997), leaving third- and higher-generation Mexican Americans trailing the education and earnings of the average American to an extent that justifiably concerns Chapa (1990).

To better understand the current and future economic prospects of Mexican Americans, we analyze in detail the intergenerational progress of Mexican-origin workers in the California and U.S. labor markets, focusing on the key issues raised by previous research. Using microdata from the CPS and the National Education Longitudinal Study (NELS), we seek to shed light on the following questions:

1. How do the education and earnings of Mexican Americans change across generations in the United States (i.e., as we compare first-generation immigrants with their second-generation children and third-generation grandchildren)?
2. Why do Mexican-origin workers earn low wages in the U.S. labor market?
3. Why do Mexican Americans, even those born in the United States, acquire less schooling than almost any other ethnic group in America?
4. In terms of educational and labor market outcomes, do Mexican Americans fare differently in California than elsewhere in the United States?

Given the large and growing presence of Mexican Americans in California's population, workforce, and schools, answers to these questions are crucial for state policy. Indeed, recent economic transformations have heightened the policy significance of the research reported here. In particular, earnings inequality and the labor market returns to various dimensions of worker skill have increased dramatically in the United States over the past two decades (Levy and Murnane, 1992; Murphy and Welch, 1992; Juhn, Murphy, and Pierce, 1993). These trends have been even more prominent in California, where there has been a sharper decline in income at the middle to lowest levels of the distribution (Reed, Haber, and Mameesh, 1996; Reed, 1999; Betts, 2000). The low levels of education and other skills possessed by Mexican-origin workers make them especially vulnerable to these ongoing changes in the wage structure. As a result, it is imperative to understand how the economic opportunities available to California's Mexican population evolve across generations. Equally important, we need to know why high school dropout rates remain stubbornly high for Mexican Americans even as the labor market prospects for less-educated workers become more and more limited.[3]

Our study proceeds as follows. Using 1996–1999 data from the CPS, the next two chapters describe the economic situation of Mexican Americans in California and the United States. Chapter 2 documents the substantial educational disadvantage of Mexican Americans, and Chapter 3 shows that this schooling deficit is the principal reason why Mexican-origin workers earn low wages. In Chapter 4, we analyze NELS data to examine in detail the determinants of racial and ethnic differences in a key educational outcome: high school graduation. Chapter 5 summarizes our findings and highlights the potential implications for public policy.

---

[3]Reyes (2001) provides a wealth of descriptive information on economic and social outcomes for Mexicans and other racial/ethnic groups in California.

2. Educational Patterns

In this and the following chapter, we use the latest available data to describe the economic situation of Mexican Americans in California and the United States. This chapter highlights the low schooling level of this group, even U.S.-born Mexican Americans, and the following chapter shows that this education deficit is primarily responsible for the relatively low wages earned by Mexican-origin workers in the U.S. labor market. In both chapters, we explore patterns of intergenerational progress, using comparisons between Mexican immigrants, the U.S.-born children of Mexican immigrants, and the later generations of Mexican Americans.

Data

In this chapter and the next, we analyze microdata from the 1996–1999 outgoing rotation group (ORG) files of the CPS. The CPS is a monthly survey of about 50,000 households that the U.S. government uses to estimate unemployment rates and other indicators of labor market activity. In addition to the detailed demographic and labor force data reported for all respondents, the CPS collects earnings information from one-quarter of the sample. The data we analyze come from these monthly earnings samples.[1]

Unlike the decennial Census, which in 1980 began collecting birthplace information only for the respondent, recent CPS data also report the countries of birth of the respondent's parents. With the CPS data, we can distinguish between three generation groups. The first generation consists of immigrants: foreign-born individuals whose parents were also born outside the United States. The second generation includes U.S.-born individuals who have at least one foreign-born parent. The designation "third and higher generation" applies to U.S. natives

---

[1]The CPS data come from national probability samples, and all of the calculations we report in this chapter and the next make use of the CPS sampling weights.

whose parents are also natives.[2] For ease of exposition, we will often refer to this last group as the "3rd+ generation" or simply the third generation.[3]

Before turning to the empirical analysis, let us mention a few issues that may affect interpretation of the intergenerational comparisons reported here. First, our intergenerational comparisons are cross-sectional because they do not attempt to match immigrant parents with their U.S.-born children who enter the labor market a couple of decades later. Instead, we compare first-, second-, and third-generation Mexican Americans at a single point in time (1996–1999). An alternative approach would be to use data from successive time periods and compare immigrant adults in some initial period with their grown-up descendants 20 or more years later. Each approach has advantages and disadvantages. One benefit of the cross-sectional approach is that using data from a single time period holds constant the social and economic environment, whereas the alternative approach can give misleading results when conditions change over time. For example, the civil rights movement may have generated economic gains for *all* generations of Mexican Americans over the 1970s and 1980s. If so, then the improvements in education and earnings observed between Mexican immigrants in the 1960s and their U.S.-born children in the 1990s would overstate the amount of progress that is solely due to being a second-generation Mexican who grew up in the United States, rather than a first-generation Mexican who grew up south of the border.

On the other hand, Borjas (1993) cautions that cross-sectional comparisons of generations can be misleading if there are important skill differences between immigrant cohorts and these differences are at least partially transmitted to the U.S.-born children of immigrants. In particular, there is evidence that recent cohorts of Mexican immigrants

---

[2]A few individuals were born abroad of American parents. We treat these individuals as U.S. natives, because they automatically receive U.S. citizenship as the children of Americans. Therefore, these individuals are assigned to our so-called "third generation" category consisting of U.S. natives whose parents are also natives.

[3]For Mexicans, this group consists primarily of individuals who are indeed third generation, whereas among non-Hispanic whites, most people we refer to as third generation actually belong to higher generations (Borjas, 1994, Tables 1 and 2).

came to the United States with fewer skills than preceding cohorts (Borjas, 1995). Consequently, cross-sectional comparisons between first- and second-generation Mexican Americans may exaggerate the amount of intergenerational progress, because second-generation Mexican Americans currently in the labor market inherited their abilities and skills from earlier immigrant cohorts who were more successful than the immigrant cohorts now at work are likely to be. For the same reason, cross-sectional comparisons between second- and third-generation Mexican Americans may be biased in favor of the third generation, although this presumes that the skill decline observed for postwar cohorts of Mexican immigrants continues back well into the first half of the 20th century.

Selective return migration can produce similar biases. If, for example, unsuccessful immigrants have a greater tendency to return eventually to their home country, then as an immigrant arrival cohort ages in the United States, it becomes increasingly represented by more successful, higher-earning individuals. This process can generate inflated estimates of immigrant labor market assimilation and might also distort intergenerational comparisons, to the extent that the children of immigrants who remain here inherit some of their parents' selectivity. Available evidence on the selectivity of return migration is mixed, however. Overall, most research suggests that the least successful immigrants are most likely to leave the United States (Borjas, 1989; Hu, 1999; Lubotsky, 2000), but Jasso and Rosenzweig (1988) find the opposite. Of greatest relevance for the current study, Hu (1999) reports that return migration selectivity is important for non-Hispanic immigrants but not for Hispanic immigrants, whereas Reyes (1997) finds that the least-educated and lowest-paid immigrants from western Mexico are most likely to return.

Another issue is that ethnic identification is to some extent endogenous, especially among people at least one or two generations removed from immigration to the United States (Waters, 1990). Consequently, the descendants of Mexican immigrants who continue to identify themselves as Mexican-origin in the third and higher generations may be a select group. In particular, if the most successful Mexican Americans are more likely to intermarry or for other reasons cease to identify themselves or their children as Hispanic, then available data may understate human capital and earnings gains between the second and third generations. Although outside the scope of the current report, an important question for future research is whether this phenomenon can explain why the economic progress of Mexican Americans appears to stall after the second generation.

To set the stage for our analysis, Tables 2.1 and 2.2 show how the population varies by race/ethnicity and generation in the 1996–1999 CPS data, both for the nation as a whole and separately for California. These calculations are for men and women ages 15 and older.[4] The racial/ethnic categories are defined to be mutually exclusive.[5]

For the United States as a whole, non-Hispanic whites compose almost three-quarters of the population, with the largest minority groups being blacks (12 percent) and Hispanics (10 percent). Asians and Native Americans represent much smaller segments of the U.S. population. Among Hispanics, Mexican Americans are the dominant subgroup, comprising over 60 percent of all Hispanics in the United States.

In California, Hispanics constitute more than one-quarter of the population, and Asians also account for a sizable share (12 percent). Over 80 percent of California's Hispanics are of Mexican descent, implying that one in five Californians is Mexican American. Other Hispanics in California originate primarily from Central and South America (representing 14 percent of California's Hispanic population and 4 percent of the overall California population).

---

[4]The calculations in Table 2.1 are based on a sample of 1,139,207 individuals for the entire United States, with 94,301 of these individuals residing in California. The sample sizes for Table 2.2 are 878,980 whites, 110,877 blacks, and 56,054 Mexicans for the entire United States, and 50,595 whites, 6,018 blacks, and 20,096 Mexicans for California alone.

[5]Like the Census, the CPS has separate questions regarding race and "Spanish origin." We label as Hispanic any respondents who indicate membership in a Spanish-origin group, and we further designate as Mexican those who choose one of the Spanish-origin categories "Mexican American," "Chicano," or "Mexican (Mexicano)." Non-Hispanics are assigned an ethnic category on the basis of their response to the race question. Therefore, our categorization of "ethnic" groups is really a categorization of "racial/ethnic" groups, but we will use the terms "ethnic" or "ethnicity" as shorthand for this categorization.

Table 2.1

Race/Ethnicity Among Men and Women Ages 15 and Older, United States and California

Racial/Ethnic Group	% of U.S. Population	% of California Population
White	73.9	54.3
Black	11.6	6.5
Native American	0.7	0.8
Asian	3.6	11.8
Hispanic	10.1	26.6
Total	100.0	100.0

Hispanic Group	% of U.S. Hispanics	% of California Hispanics
Mexican	62.1	81.1
Puerto Rican	10.1	1.1
Cuban	5.0	0.8
Central/South American	15.4	13.8
Other Hispanic	7.4	3.2
Total	100.0	100.0

SOURCE: 1996–1999 CPS ORG data.

NOTE: Numbers in the tables throughout this report may not sum to 100.0 percent because of rounding.

Table 2.2

Race/Ethnicity and Generation Among Men and Women Ages 15 and Older, United States and California (in percent)

Racial/Ethnic Group	Recent Immigrant	Earlier Immigrant	2nd Generation	3rd+ Generation	Total
United States					
Whites	1.3	2.8	8.6	87.2	100.0
Blacks	2.8	4.1	2.3	90.8	100.0
Mexican Americans	21.3	27.6	22.2	28.9	100.0
California					
Whites	2.8	6.2	12.0	79.0	100.0
Blacks	2.4	3.0	2.6	92.0	100.0
Mexican Americans	21.9	35.2	23.5	19.5	100.0

SOURCE: 1996–1999 CPS ORG data.

NOTE: Recent immigrants are defined as those who arrived in the United States within approximately 10 years of the survey date.

In this report, we study the Mexican-origin population, and for comparison purposes we include whites and blacks in the analyses. Table 2.2 presents the distribution of the population across generations for these three racial/ethnic groups. We split the first generation into "recent immigrants" who have been in the United States for 10 years or less and "earlier immigrants" who have spent more than 10 years here. This table reveals that the overwhelming majority of Mexican Americans come from families that have been in this country for no more than two generations. In particular, about half of Mexican Americans are foreign-born and another fifth have at least one immigrant parent. By contrast, only 13 percent of whites and 9 percent of blacks are of the first or second generation. The pattern is similar but accentuated in California, where the Mexican American population has a larger proportion of earlier immigrants and a smaller proportion of third-generation individuals than in the entire United States. Among whites, California also has higher population shares in the first and second generations than does the nation as a whole.

In addition to being dominated by immigrants and the sons and daughters of immigrants, the Mexican-origin population in the United States has another important feature—its geographic concentration. California is the state of residence for 41 percent of Mexican Americans in the United States and Texas is home to another 30 percent. Therefore, over 70 percent of the Mexican-origin population in the United States lives in just two states. If we also include the sizable clusters of Mexican Americans residing in Arizona, Illinois, Colorado, and New Mexico, we find that more than 85 percent of the Mexican American population is concentrated in six states.[6] To explore geographic variation in Mexican American outcomes, many of the analyses presented below for the United States as a whole are also reported for the following three regions: California, Texas, and the remainder of the country. However, our discussion focuses on the results for the entire United States, because these results are based on the largest samples and also because the region-specific results can be affected by selective migration within the United States. If, for example, second-

---

[6]These statistics were calculated using the same data that underlie Table 2.1.

and later-generation Mexican Americans tend to move away from the enclaves favored by Mexican immigrants, then intergenerational comparisons of those Mexican Americans confined to a particular state such as California or Texas might yield misleading patterns.

Educational Outcomes

Tables 2.3 to 2.6 examine educational attainment, which is a key determinant of how workers fare in the U.S. labor market.[7] We here limit the sample to individuals ages 25–59, and we report separate calculations for men and women. These tables show average completed years of schooling, as well as the distribution of the population across various mutually exclusive and exhaustive education categories.[8] Mexican Americans are disaggregated by generation, and comparable statistics are presented for third-generation whites and blacks. Third-generation whites provide a yardstick for measuring Mexican American outcomes against those of the primary native "majority" group in American society, and third-generation blacks are an important native "minority" group that is instructive to compare with Mexican Americans.

Table 2.3 reports these education statistics for the United States as a whole. The patterns for men and women are similar. First, the educational attainment of Mexican immigrants is strikingly low. Foreign-born Mexican immigrants possess on average only about eight and a half years of schooling, with over 65 percent of this population lacking a high school diploma and less than 5 percent having completed

---

[7]Sample sizes for the gender, race/ethnicity, and generation cells in Tables 2.3 to 2.6 are reported in Appendix Table A.1. For the United States as a whole, the sample sizes are large, yielding precise estimates of outcomes. In the top half of Table 2.3, for example, sample sizes for the various generations of Mexican men range from 2,500 to 6,500. The sample size is 25,000 for third-generation black men and over 200,000 for third-generation white men. The sample sizes for women are similar. Of course, sample sizes are smaller for subregions of the United States.

[8]In CPS data, the category "high school graduate" includes those who completed high school by means of an equivalency exam (such as the General Equivalency Diploma, or GED) in addition to those who followed the traditional route of taking a set of courses that culminates in graduation at the end of twelfth grade. The category "postgraduate degree" represents those who completed college and subsequently earned a graduate or professional degree.

Table 2.3

Educational Attainment, by Race/Ethnicity and Generation, Ages 25–59, U.S. Total

Education Level	Mexican Americans				3rd+ Generation Whites	3rd+ Generation Blacks
	Recent Immigrant	Earlier Immigrant	2nd Generation	3rd+ Generation		
Men						
Avg. years of education	8.6	8.4	11.9	12.2	13.6	12.6
Percentage with						
8 years or less	46.2	48.3	11.1	7.0	1.9	3.1
Some high school	20.1	18.9	15.5	16.5	6.8	13.5
High school graduate	20.0	19.9	33.9	38.6	33.3	40.8
Some college	8.0	9.1	27.2	26.1	27.1	28.1
Bachelor's degree	4.1	2.9	8.3	8.8	20.7	11.0
Postgraduate degree	1.7	1.0	4.0	3.0	10.3	3.7
Total	100.0	100.0	100.0	100.0	100.0	100.0
Women						
Avg. years of education	8.2	8.5	11.9	12.0	13.5	12.8
Percentage with						
8 years or less	51.3	47.7	11.9	8.3	1.4	2.4
Some high school	18.9	18.8	15.1	16.7	5.9	13.3
High school graduate	17.3	19.1	32.7	37.2	34.6	36.7
Some college	7.6	10.7	28.4	27.7	29.6	31.1
Bachelor's degree	3.7	3.1	8.6	7.6	20.0	11.9
Postgraduate degree	1.2	0.7	3.3	2.5	8.5	4.6
Total	100.0	100.0	100.0	100.0	100.0	100.0

SOURCE: 1996–1999 CPS ORG data.

NOTE: Recent immigrants are defined as those who arrived in the United States within approximately 10 years of the survey date.

college. Second, enormous educational improvement takes place between first- and second-generation Mexican Americans. Indeed, average schooling levels are about three and a half years higher for the second generation than for Mexican immigrants. Therefore, a large portion of the overall education deficit for Mexican Americans derives from the presence of large numbers of Mexican immigrants with very low education levels. The U.S.-born children of Mexican immigrants close most but not all of this education gap.

Finally, intergenerational progress in schooling among Mexican Americans appears to slow considerably after the second generation. The modest education gains observed between the second and third generations are largely attributable to the third generation having a lower proportion with less than nine years of schooling and a higher proportion of high school graduates. Nevertheless, the educational attainment of third- and higher-generation Mexican Americans trails that of non-Hispanics by an alarming amount. Within the third generation, Mexican Americans average a year and a half less schooling than whites, are three times as likely to not complete high school (roughly 24 percent for Mexican Americans versus 8 percent for whites), and are about one-third as likely to earn a bachelor's degree (roughly 11 percent for Mexican Americans versus 30 percent for whites). Compared to blacks, third-generation Mexican Americans average 0.4 fewer years of schooling among men and 0.8 fewer years of schooling among women. Mexican Americans are also more likely than blacks to not finish high school (24 percent versus 16 percent) and have lower rates of college completion (11 percent versus 15 percent). Consequently, the educational attainment of U.S.-born Mexican Americans is low not just in comparison with the white majority but also in comparison with disadvantaged minority groups such as native blacks.

Tables 2.4–2.6 present these same education statistics for California, Texas, and the rest of the United States. Although the schooling levels of U.S.-born Mexican Americans are lower in Texas than elsewhere, the general patterns described above for the entire United States also show up in each of the regions. Everywhere, Mexican Americans experience huge educational gains between the first and second generations but little further improvement after the second generation, leaving substantial

Table 2.4

Educational Attainment, by Race/Ethnicity and Generation, Ages 25–59, California

Education Level	Mexican Americans Recent Immigrant	Mexican Americans Earlier Immigrant	Mexican Americans 2nd Generation	Mexican Americans 3rd+ Generation	3rd+ Generation Whites	3rd+ Generation Blacks
Men						
Avg. years of education	8.4	8.4	12.4	12.5	14.1	13.3
Percentage with						
8 years or less	47.2	47.9	7.5	3.5	0.6	0.9
Some high school	20.8	19.1	14.0	14.0	4.6	7.5
High school graduate	19.6	19.9	33.7	40.5	22.9	31.6
Some college	8.5	9.7	30.5	30.9	34.2	38.5
Bachelor's degree	2.9	2.7	9.8	8.3	25.0	17.1
Postgraduate degree	1.0	0.7	4.6	2.8	12.7	4.4
Total	100.0	100.0	100.0	100.0	100.0	100.0
Women						
Avg. years of education	7.8	8.3	12.2	12.3	13.9	13.4
Percentage with						
8 years or less	55.2	48.9	8.3	4.1	0.4	0.7
Some high school	18.0	19.0	14.0	18.0	4.4	7.7
High school graduate	16.0	18.7	33.4	35.4	25.3	26.4
Some college	7.5	10.3	32.2	31.8	36.9	43.3
Bachelor's degree	2.4	2.8	9.0	7.4	23.6	15.8
Postgraduate degree	1.0	0.4	3.2	3.2	9.4	6.0
Total	100.0	100.0	100.0	100.0	100.0	100.0

SOURCE: 1996–1999 CPS ORG data.

NOTE: Recent immigrants are defined as those who arrived in the United States within approximately 10 years of the survey date.

Table 2.5

Educational Attainment, by Race/Ethnicity and Generation, Ages 25–59, Texas

Education Level	Mexican Americans				3rd+ Generation Whites	3rd+ Generation Blacks
	Recent Immigrant	Earlier Immigrant	2nd Generation	3rd+ Generation		
Men						
Avg. years of education	8.8	8.2	11.4	11.8	13.8	12.9
Percentage with						
8 years or less	47.2	48.6	15.6	10.1	1.3	1.2
Some high school	18.2	18.9	18.4	18.3	5.6	9.9
High school graduate	16.9	19.4	32.0	39.4	28.2	39.7
Some college	7.5	8.3	25.8	22.3	29.6	32.5
Bachelor's degree	7.3	2.8	6.2	7.7	24.7	12.9
Postgraduate degree	3.0	2.1	2.1	2.3	10.7	3.8
Total	100.0	100.0	100.0	100.0	100.0	100.0
Women						
Avg. years of education	8.6	8.4	11.3	11.7	13.6	12.9
Percentage with						
8 years or less	47.8	49.2	17.9	11.5	1.1	1.4
Some high school	21.9	18.3	16.9	17.7	6.0	11.7
High school graduate	15.9	18.4	31.1	38.0	30.2	36.3
Some college	6.8	9.5	23.2	23.8	32.1	34.1
Bachelor's degree	5.5	3.6	7.7	7.2	22.8	11.9
Postgraduate degree	2.2	1.0	3.2	1.8	7.8	4.5
Total	100.0	100.0	100.0	100.0	100.0	100.0

SOURCE: 1996–1999 CPS ORG data.

NOTE: Recent immigrants are defined as those who arrived in the United States within approximately 10 years of the survey date.

Table 2.6

Educational Attainment, by Race/Ethnicity and Generation, Ages 25–59, United States Excluding California and Texas

Education Level	Mexican Americans				3rd+ Generation Whites	3rd+ Generation Blacks
	Recent Immigrant	Earlier Immigrant	2nd Generation	3rd+ Generation		
Men						
Avg. years of education	8.8	8.4	12.1	12.4	13.5	12.5
Percentage with						
8 years or less	44.9	48.7	10.9	6.0	2.1	3.4
Some high school	20.2	18.6	14.3	16.1	7.0	14.3
High school graduate	21.5	20.2	36.5	35.6	34.6	41.7
Some college	7.7	8.4	24.4	27.2	26.2	26.7
Bachelor's degree	3.9	3.4	8.6	11.1	20.0	10.2
Postgraduate degree	1.9	0.8	5.4	4.0	10.1	3.6
Total	100.0	100.0	100.0	100.0	100.0	100.0
Women						
Avg. years of education	8.5	9.0	12.1	12.2	13.5	12.8
Percentage with						
8 years or less	48.3	43.6	9.8	7.5	1.5	2.6
Some high school	18.7	18.7	14.7	14.0	6.1	13.9
High school graduate	19.5	20.6	33.7	37.6	35.8	37.5
Some college	8.0	12.8	29.2	29.7	28.7	29.9
Bachelor's degree	4.5	3.1	8.9	8.3	19.5	11.6
Postgraduate degree	1.1	1.2	3.7	2.9	8.5	4.6
Total	100.0	100.0	100.0	100.0	100.0	100.0

SOURCE: 1996–1999 CPS ORG data.

NOTE: Recent immigrants are defined as those who arrived in the United States within approximately 10 years of the survey date.

schooling deficits for third-generation Mexican Americans relative to whites or blacks. In fact, the average schooling gaps between third-generation Mexican Americans and blacks are particularly large (on the order of a year) in California and Texas, the two states where most Mexican Americans live.

The relatively modest amount of educational progress observed between second- and third-generation Mexican Americans is a puzzle for the following reason. Previous studies have consistently found parental education to be one of the most important determinants of an individual's educational attainment and ultimate labor market success (Haveman and Wolfe, 1994). Through this mechanism, the huge educational gain between first- and second-generation Mexican Americans should produce a sizable jump in schooling between the second and third generations, because on average the third generation has parents who are much better educated than those of the second generation. Yet the improvement in schooling we expect to find between the second and third generations is largely absent. We will return to this puzzle in Chapter 4, where we examine in detail the determinants of educational outcomes.

3. Labor Market Success

In this chapter, we explore the extent and determinants of earnings differences between Mexican Americans, whites, and blacks. Our focus is on hourly earnings because previous research indicates that the income disadvantage of Mexican-origin households stems primarily from low wages rather than from low rates of labor force participation, high rates of unemployment, or reduced workweeks (Abowd and Killingsworth, 1984; Borjas, 1984; Reimers, 1984; Bean and Tienda, 1987). We show that the educational disadvantage of Mexican Americans documented in the previous chapter is the principal reason why average wages are low for Mexican-origin workers in the U.S. labor market.

Data

We begin with the same data analyzed in the preceding chapter: 1996–1999 CPS samples of Mexican American, third-generation white, and third-generation black men and women ages 25–59. Because earnings information is available only for those with jobs, we must now further limit the sample to individuals who were employed during the CPS survey week. To give an idea how this affects the samples, Table 3.1 reports employment rates for the relevant groups.[1]

Among men, employment rates approach 90 percent for Mexican immigrants, similar to the rates for third-generation whites. The employment rates of U.S.-born Mexican American men tend to be a few percentage points lower than this but substantially higher than the corresponding rates for black men. For women, employment rates are around 70 percent for U.S.-born Mexican Americans and for blacks,

---

[1]Table 3.1 is based on the same data used in Tables 2.3 to 2.6. Sample sizes for the relevant gender, race/ethnicity, and generation cells are reported in Appendix Table A.1. Self-employed workers remain in these samples used to compare education levels and employment rates, but, as explained below, by necessity they are excluded from the samples used to analyze wages.

Table 3.1

Percentage Employed During Survey Week, by Race/Ethnicity and Generation, Ages 25–59

Race/Ethnicity/Generation	U.S. Total	California	Texas	United States Excluding California and Texas
Men				
Mexican Americans				
Recent immigrant	90.1	88.7	90.9	91.0
Earlier immigrant	87.3	86.0	88.3	89.3
2nd generation	84.9	84.3	84.1	86.7
3rd+ generation	85.1	81.4	86.8	86.3
3rd+ generation whites	89.3	87.7	91.5	89.3
3rd+ generation blacks	77.1	73.6	82.9	77.0
Women				
Mexican Americans				
Recent immigrant	40.0	41.6	36.3	40.0
Earlier immigrant	53.0	53.2	50.7	54.8
2nd generation	68.0	71.4	62.4	69.8
3rd+ generation	69.1	67.5	68.5	71.5
3rd+ generation whites	75.0	73.4	74.6	75.2
3rd+ generation blacks	70.9	67.2	75.0	70.8

SOURCE: 1996–1999 CPS ORG data.

NOTE: Recent immigrants are defined as those who arrived in the United States within approximately 10 years of the survey date.

with somewhat higher rates for whites and much lower rates for Mexican immigrants.

The fact that earnings information is unavailable for those without jobs can distort wage comparisons such as those we make in this chapter. For example, suppose that individuals with lower earnings potential are less likely to be employed than those with higher skills and better labor market opportunities. In this case, the average wages we observe, in the sample of people with jobs, are higher than they would be if we somehow had earnings data for all individuals, including those without jobs. Most important, the upward bias to average wages will be bigger for groups with relatively low employment rates, such as black men and Mexican-born women, because for these groups a larger share of potentially low-wage individuals will be excluded from the earnings sample. To mitigate this problem, we present wage comparisons that control for observable indicators of skill such as education and age, but the problem remains to the extent that there exist other important, unobserved determinants of labor market skills and wages that are correlated with employment rates. This point should be kept in mind when interpreting the results reported below.[2]

The basic monthly CPS does not collect earnings information from self-employed workers, and therefore only so-called "wage and salary" employees are included in the wage analyses.[3] For each worker, hourly earnings are computed as the ratio of usual weekly earnings to usual weekly hours of work. Workers with computed hourly wages below $1 or above $500 are considered outliers and excluded. Finally, to ensure that workers satisfy a minimum level of labor force attachment, the wage analyses include only those who work at least 10 hours per week.[4]

Wage Comparisons

Multiple regression provides a convenient way to systematically investigate the influence of various factors on wage differences between race/ethnicity/generation groups. For the United States as a whole, Table 3.2 reports the results of hourly wage regressions, estimated by ordinary least squares, that show how minority-white wage gaps change as control variables are added in succession. Separate regressions were run for men and women. These regressions allow intercepts to differ across race/ethnicity/generation groups (with third-generation whites as the reference group), but other coefficients are restricted to be the same for all groups. The dependent variable is the natural logarithm of hourly earnings, so the estimated coefficients on the race/ethnicity/generation

---

[2]Under certain circumstances, statistical techniques can be used to adjust wage averages for the effects of employment differences across groups (Heckman, 1979), but the CPS data that we analyze here do not provide the information necessary to make credible adjustments of this type.

[3]Self-employment rates are lower for Mexican Americans and blacks than for whites (Bean et al., 2001, Table 21). Therefore, self-employment selectivity has the potential to distort wage comparisons in the manner described in the preceding paragraph.

[4]Sample sizes for our CPS wage analyses are reported in Appendix Table A.2.

Table 3.2

Log Hourly Wage Differentials, Relative to 3rd+ Generation Whites, by Race/Ethnicity and Generation, Ages 25–59, U.S. Total

Race/Ethnicity/Generation	Men			Women		
	(1)	(2)	(3)	(1)	(2)	(3)
Mexican Americans						
Recent immigrant	−.757	−.662	−.357	−.696	−.665	−.297
Earlier immigrant	−.564	−.554	−.240	−.547	−.546	−.205
2nd generation	−.273	−.239	−.110	−.228	−.212	−.074
3rd+ generation	−.264	−.243	−.116	−.222	−.216	−.077
3rd+ generation blacks	−.289	−.282	−.210	−.160	−.158	−.090
Controls for						
Survey month/year	Yes	Yes	Yes	Yes	Yes	Yes
Geographic location	Yes	Yes	Yes	Yes	Yes	Yes
Age	No	Yes	Yes	No	Yes	Yes
Education level	No	No	Yes	No	No	Yes

SOURCE: 1996–1999 CPS ORG data.

NOTE: The reported figures are estimated coefficients from ordinary least squares regressions in which the dependent variable is the natural logarithm of average hourly earnings. Recent immigrants are defined as those who arrived in the United States within approximately 10 years of the survey date.

indicator variables represent approximate percentage wage differentials between each group and third-generation whites.[5]

In the first regression specification—the columns labeled (1) in Table 3.2—the control variables include indicators for the month and year of the CPS survey that the observation comes from and also a vector of geographic variables.[6] In effect, these estimates provide wage comparisons at a single point in time between workers who live in the same place, as a way of standardizing for intertemporal and interregional

---

[5]For ease of exposition, we will refer to log wage differences as if they represent percentage wage differentials. Strictly speaking, however, log wage differences closely approximate percentage wage differentials only when the log wage differences are on the order of .25 or less in absolute value. For larger differences, the implied percentage wage differential can be calculated as $e^c - 1$, where c is the log wage difference (i.e., the estimated coefficient on the relevant ethnicity/generation indicator variable).

[6]The geographic controls are indicators for metropolitan status (central city, elsewhere in a metropolitan statistical area, not in a metropolitan statistical area, and metropolitan status not identified), the nine Census divisions, and the states of California and Texas.

variation in the cost-of-living and labor market conditions.[7] Among men, average wages are virtually the same for second- and third-generation Mexican Americans, with both groups earning about 27 percent less than third-generation whites, which is similar to the corresponding wage deficit of 29 percent for blacks. Average wages are much lower for Mexican immigrants. The implication is that Mexican Americans enjoy wage growth of 30 percent or more between the first and second generations. Intergenerational progress appears to stall after the second generation, however, as no further wage growth is evident between the second and third generations, despite the substantial wage gap that persists between U.S.-born Mexican Americans and whites. The patterns for women are similar, except that the wage deficit of blacks (16 percent) is lower than the 22 percent deficit for U.S.-born Mexican Americans.

In the second regression specification—the columns labeled (2) in Table 3.2—we control for age by adding a set of indicator variables identifying the five-year age cohort to which each worker belongs. Other than attenuating somewhat the male wage gap for recent Mexican immigrants, who tend to be young, controlling for age has only a minor effect on the wage differentials.

In the final regression specification—the columns labeled (3) in Table 3.2—we add a set of indicator variables for educational attainment, using the same six schooling categories that we employed in

---

[7]Standard errors indicate how precisely regression coefficients are estimated. Sampling error arises because estimates are calculated using samples that represent only a small fraction of the underlying population. If the only source of error is sampling error (as opposed to other types of error that impart systematic bias), then the chances are about 95 percent that the true coefficient is within two standard errors (plus or minus) of its estimate. An estimated coefficient is said to be "statistically significant" when it is at least twice the size of its standard error, because this makes it unlikely that the true coefficient is zero. In tables, standard errors are often displayed in parentheses below the corresponding coefficient. To avoid clutter, however, we will omit standard errors from most of the tables in this report. Instead, Appendix A reports standard errors for those regression coefficients whose standard errors are not displayed in the same table. For example, Appendix Table A.3 provides standard errors for the estimates in Table 3.2. Note that all of the minority-white wage gaps in Table 3.2 are statistically significant.

Tables 2.3 to 2.6.[8] Controlling for education shrinks the wage deficit (relative to third-generation whites) for all groups but much more so for Mexican Americans than for blacks. Among men, the wage gap for U.S.-born Mexican Americans is more than halved (from 24 percent to 11 percent) as we move from specification (2) to specification (3), whereas the corresponding wage gap for blacks falls by only one-quarter (from 28 percent to 21 percent). Among women, the wage gap declines by almost two-thirds for U.S.-born Mexican Americans (from 21 percent to 8 percent) but by less than half for blacks (from 16 percent to 9 percent). These results highlight the prominent role that education plays in accounting for the relatively low wages earned by Mexican-origin workers in the United States.

The estimates in Table 3.2 also imply that education is a key determinant of the substantial wage differential between Mexican immigrants and U.S.-born Mexican Americans. For both men and women, the wage gap of more than 30 percent observed in column (2) between earlier immigrants and the second generation shrinks to just 13 percent in column (3). This pattern indicates that much of the wage progress across generations for Mexican Americans is driven by the intergenerational improvements in schooling that we documented in the previous chapter.

After simultaneously controlling for geographic location, age, and education, the remaining wage deficit of 11 percent for second- and third-generation Mexican men is much smaller than the 21 percent wage deficit of black men. For women, the analogous wage deficits are similar for the two groups (8 percent for U.S.-born Mexican Americans and 9 percent for blacks). These findings suggest that differences in labor market skills, as measured by crude indicators such as age and especially years of schooling, account for a large portion of the wage gaps between U.S.-born Mexican Americans and whites.

Tables 3.3 to 3.5 repeat this analysis for each of the three regions. In general, the same patterns arise as for the United States as a whole, with

---

[8]The six mutually exclusive and exhaustive education categories are as follows: eight years or less, some high school, high school graduate, some college, bachelor's degree, and postgraduate degree.

Table 3.3

Log Hourly Wage Differentials, Relative to 3rd+ Generation Whites, by Race/Ethnicity and Generation, Ages 25–59, California

Race/Ethnicity/Generation	Men			Women		
	(1)	(2)	(3)	(1)	(2)	(3)
Mexican Americans						
Recent immigrant	−.862	−.752	−.403	−.799	−.759	−.346
Earlier immigrant	−.640	−.626	−.275	−.612	−.607	−.235
2nd generation	−.263	−.210	−.077	−.258	−.236	−.081
3rd+ generation	−.270	−.249	−.111	−.216	−.208	−.064
3rd+ generation blacks	−.300	−.286	−.236	−.135	−.132	−.100
Controls for						
Survey month/year	Yes	Yes	Yes	Yes	Yes	Yes
Geographic location	Yes	Yes	Yes	Yes	Yes	Yes
Age	No	Yes	Yes	No	Yes	Yes
Education level	No	No	Yes	No	No	Yes

SOURCE: 1996–1999 CPS ORG data.

NOTE: The reported figures are estimated coefficients from ordinary least squares regressions in which the dependent variable is the natural logarithm of average hourly earnings. Recent immigrants are defined as those who arrived in the United States within approximately 10 years of the survey date.

Table 3.4

Log Hourly Wage Differentials, Relative to 3rd+ Generation Whites, by Race/Ethnicity and Generation, Ages 25–59, Texas

Race/Ethnicity/Generation	Men			Women		
	(1)	(2)	(3)	(1)	(2)	(3)
Mexican Americans						
Recent immigrant	−.731	−.668	−.372	−.698	−.683	−.332
Earlier immigrant	−.572	−.565	−.246	−.571	−.571	−.231
2nd generation	−.387	−.371	−.198	−.288	−.275	−.120
3rd+ generation	−.372	−.352	−.181	−.321	−.317	−.148
3rd+ generation blacks	−.314	−.297	−.222	−.179	−.173	−.100
Controls for						
Survey month/year	Yes	Yes	Yes	Yes	Yes	Yes
Geographic location	Yes	Yes	Yes	Yes	Yes	Yes
Age	No	Yes	Yes	No	Yes	Yes
Education level	No	No	Yes	No	No	Yes

SOURCE: 1996–1999 CPS ORG data.

NOTE: The reported figures are estimated coefficients from ordinary least squares regressions in which the dependent variable is the natural logarithm of average hourly earnings. Recent immigrants are defined as those who arrived in the United States within approximately 10 years of the survey date.

Table 3.5

Log Hourly Wage Differentials, Relative to 3rd+ Generation Whites, by Race/Ethnicity and Generation, Ages 25–59, United States Excluding California and Texas

Race/Ethnicity/Generation	Men			Women		
	(1)	(2)	(3)	(1)	(2)	(3)
Mexican Americans						
Recent immigrant	−.699	−.604	−.317	−.570	−.539	−.207
Earlier immigrant	−.481	−.470	−.173	−.417	−.415	−.105
2nd generation	−.227	−.198	−.086	−.151	−.140	−.027
3rd+ generation	−.177	−.157	−.060	−.140	−.135	−.020
3rd+ generation blacks	−.284	−.278	−.206	−.157	−.155	−.086
Controls for						
Survey month/year	Yes	Yes	Yes	Yes	Yes	Yes
Geographic location	Yes	Yes	Yes	Yes	Yes	Yes
Age	No	Yes	Yes	No	Yes	Yes
Education level	No	No	Yes	No	No	Yes

SOURCE: 1996–1999 CPS ORG data.

NOTE: The reported figures are estimated coefficients from ordinary least squares regressions in which the dependent variable is the natural logarithm of average hourly earnings. Recent immigrants are defined as those who arrived in the United States within approximately 10 years of the survey date.

two main exceptions. First, the wage gaps for U.S.-born Mexican Americans are larger in Texas than elsewhere. Second, after controlling for both age and education in specification (3), remaining wage gaps in Texas for U.S.-born Mexican Americans are similar to those for blacks, whereas in California and the rest of the country, these wage gaps are smaller for Mexican Americans than for blacks.

Wage Determinants

The wage comparisons presented in Tables 3.2 to 3.5 are informative and easy to interpret, but they are also quite restrictive because they constrain the wage structure to be the same, except for intercept differences, across race/ethnicity/generation groups. We now relax this restriction and allow the wage effects of age and education to vary by race/ethnicity and generation.[9] By estimating group-specific returns for

---

[9]We continue to restrict the coefficients of the survey month/year and geographic indicators to be the same across groups. These variables are included to control for

potential work experience and schooling, we can examine how the determinants of hourly earnings differ across groups.

For simplicity, we initially specify education as a continuous variable representing completed years of schooling. Given this "linear" specification of education and the logarithmic specification of hourly earnings as the dependent variable, the estimated schooling coefficients measure the percentage wage boost associated with each additional year of education. Table 3.6 reports the estimated returns to education from this linear specification.

Table 3.6

Linear Returns to Education, by Race/Ethnicity and Generation, Ages 25–59

Race/Ethnicity/Generation	U.S. Total	California	Texas	United States Excluding California and Texas
Men				
Mexican Americans				
Immigrant	.032	.034	.030	.029
2nd generation	.076	.091	.072	.059
3rd+ generation	.076	.089	.075	.065
3rd+ generation whites	.084	.093	.096	.082
3rd+ generation blacks	.080	.091	.104	.078
Women				
Mexican Americans				
Immigrant	.038	.041	.045	.024
2nd generation	.080	.085	.074	.086
3rd+ generation	.104	.117	.101	.096
3rd+ generation whites	.107	.111	.107	.106
3rd+ generation blacks	.112	.130	.124	.110

SOURCE: 1996–1999 CPS ORG data.

NOTE: The reported figures are estimated coefficients on completed years of schooling from ordinary least squares regressions in which the dependent variable is the natural logarithm of average hourly earnings. These regressions also control for survey month/year, geographic location, and age.

---

differences over time and between regions in the cost-of-living and economic conditions—factors that may affect all groups to a similar extent. We also constrain the returns to age and education to be the same for all Mexican immigrants, regardless of whether they are recent or earlier arrivals. The expanded regressions are similar to specification (3) in Tables 3.2 to 3.5, with the addition of group-specific returns to age and education.

Returns to education are at least twice as high for U.S.-born Mexican Americans as for Mexican immigrants—a well-known result typically thought to reflect the advantages of U.S. schooling for the U.S. labor market (Chiswick, 1978). Among men, returns to schooling do not differ between second- and third-generation Mexican Americans. Overall, male returns to education for U.S.-born Mexican Americans (7.6 percent) are somewhat below the corresponding returns for blacks (8 percent) and whites (8.4 percent), but this pattern differs by region. For U.S.-born men, returns to schooling in California do not vary much across racial/ethnic groups, whereas in the rest of the country, returns are noticeably lower for Mexican Americans than for others. Among women, the returns to education for Mexican Americans rise for each successive generation, including a sizable jump between the second and third generations; and, in all regions, the Mexican returns are similar to those of whites by the third generation. In general, the economic payoff to additional schooling is about as high for U.S.-born Mexican Americans as for other U.S. natives, especially in California and among third- and higher-generation women. Therefore, the substantial educational disadvantage of Mexican Americans documented in the previous chapter does not appear to be driven by less-generous labor market rewards for making such human capital investments.

The estimates in Table 3.6 constrain the percentage wage gain from an additional year of schooling to be the same at all levels of education. These estimates provide a convenient summary of how returns to education differ across groups, but they may miss nonlinearities such as "sheepskin effects" in which wages rise discretely at certain educational milestones such as completing high school or college. Tables 3.7 to 3.10 address this issue by reporting the results of adopting a less restrictive specification of the returns to education. We ran regressions similar to those that underlie Table 3.6, but we replaced the completed years of schooling variable with a set of indicator variables identifying the six education categories defined previously. The estimated coefficients on these indicator variables represent the approximate percentage wage differential between workers with that particular education level and high school graduates (the reference group), holding constant geographic location and age.

The nonlinear returns to education in Tables 3.7 to 3.10 display the same patterns as the linear returns in Table 3.6. First, among both men and women, wage differentials across education categories are generally much larger for U.S.-born Mexican Americans than for Mexican immigrants, implying a lower return to schooling for immigrants. For example, the wage advantage of male high school graduates over men with at least nine years of schooling but no diploma is 13 percent among Mexican immigrants, 24 percent among second-generation Mexican Americans, and 22 percent among third-generation Mexican Americans (see Table 3.7). Second, wage differentials across education levels are roughly similar for all groups of U.S.-born men, whether they be second-

Table 3.7

Nonlinear Returns to Education, by Race/Ethnicity and Generation, Ages 25–59, U.S. Total

Education Level	Mexican Americans			3rd Generation Whites	3rd Generation Blacks
	Immigrant	2nd Generation	3rd+ Generation		
Men					
8 years or less	−.196	−.347	−.361	−.323	−.272
Some high school	−.126	−.243	−.223	−.192	−.187
High school graduate (reference group)					
Some college	.087	.179	.110	.103	.103
Bachelor's degree	.236	.434	.364	.359	.342
Postgraduate degree	.575	.527	.403	.479	.499
Women					
8 years or less	−.195	−.257	−.400	−.344	−.275
Some high school	−.149	−.209	−.287	−.225	−.231
High school graduate (reference group)					
Some college	.139	.166	.142	.159	.162
Bachelor's degree	.407	.521	.491	.444	.475
Postgraduate degree	.615	.566	.769	.632	.670

SOURCE: 1996–1999 CPS ORG data.

NOTE: The reported figures are estimated coefficients on indicators of schooling level from ordinary least squares regressions in which the dependent variable is the natural logarithm of average hourly earnings. These regressions also control for survey month/year, geographic location, and age.

Table 3.8

Nonlinear Returns to Education, by Race/Ethnicity and Generation, Ages 25–59, California

Education Level	Mexican Americans			3rd Generation Whites	3rd Generation Blacks
	Immigrant	2nd Generation	3rd+ Generation		
Men					
8 years or less	−.210	−.497	−.492	−.347	−.257
Some high school	−.121	−.305	−.223	−.258	−.264
High school graduate (reference group)					
Some college	.141	.194	.085	.129	.092
Bachelor's degree	.314	.418	.400	.403	.283
Postgraduate degree	.521	.521	.503	.523	.661
Women					
8 years or less	−.204	−.245	−.388	−.518	−.368
Some high school	−.141	−.227	−.371	−.266	−.391
High school graduate (reference group)					
Some college	.187	.206	.081	.174	.218
Bachelor's degree	.537	.510	.441	.469	.564
Postgraduate degree	.924	.498	.846	.659	.726

SOURCE: 1996–1999 CPS ORG data.

NOTE: The reported figures are estimated coefficients on indicators of schooling level from ordinary least squares regressions in which the dependent variable is the natural logarithm of average hourly earnings. These regressions also control for survey month/year, geographic location, and age.

or third-generation Mexican Americans or third-generation whites or blacks. This statement also applies to women, except that the implied returns to education are a bit lower for second-generation Mexican Americans than for other U.S.-born women. For example, among third-generation men, the wage gap between college graduates and high school graduates is 36 percent for Mexican Americans and whites and 34 percent for blacks. The corresponding wage gaps for third-generation women are 49 percent for Mexican Americans, 44 percent for whites, and 48 percent for blacks. Regional patterns (Tables 3.8 to 3.10) resemble those just described for the United States as a whole (Table 3.7).

Table 3.9

Nonlinear Returns to Education, by Race/Ethnicity and Generation, Ages 25–59, Texas

Education Level	Mexican Americans			3rd Generation Whites	3rd Generation Blacks
	Immigrant	2nd Generation	3rd+ Generation		
Men					
8 years or less	−.157	−.219	−.311	−.299	−.700
Some high school	−.126	−.115	−.214	−.222	−.187
High school graduate (reference group)					
Some college	.025	.263	.145	.122	.184
Bachelor's degree	.285	.568	.361	.430	.384
Postgraduate degree	.673	.796	.543	.538	.652
Women					
8 years or less	−.183	−.204	−.387	−.216	−.457
Some high school	−.126	−.185	−.237	−.262	−.256
High school graduate (reference group)					
Some college	.155	.198	.183	.166	.178
Bachelor's degree	.465	.592	.529	.447	.506
Postgraduate degree	.691	.672	.841	.630	.691

SOURCE: 1996–1999 CPS ORG data.

NOTE: The reported figures are estimated coefficients on indicators of schooling level from ordinary least squares regressions in which the dependent variable is the natural logarithm of average hourly earnings. These regressions also control for survey month/year, geographic location, and age.

The standard CPS education question does not distinguish among high school graduates according to whether they obtained their diploma in the usual way or through an equivalency exam such as the GED. Additional questions in the 1998 and 1999 CPS data, however, do allow us to make this distinction. To explore the effect of a GED on earnings of Mexican-origin workers, we estimated regressions like those that underlie Table 3.7, but we added an indicator variable identifying individuals in the "high school graduate" education category who

Table 3.10

Nonlinear Returns to Education, by Race/Ethnicity and Generation, Ages 25–59, United States Excluding California and Texas

	Mexican Americans			3rd Generation Whites	3rd Generation Blacks
Education Level	Immigrant	2nd Generation	3rd+ Generation		
Men					
8 years or less	−.200	−.311	−.402	−.325	−.267
Some high school	−.132	−.244	−.241	−.186	−.187
High school graduate (reference group)					
Some college	.058	.077	.077	.100	.097
Bachelor's degree	.104	.326	.313	.351	.350
Postgraduate degree	.531	.380	.166	.473	.473
Women					
8 years or less	−.160	−.365	−.359	−.347	−.266
Some high school	−.154	−.198	−.283	−.221	−.228
High school graduate (reference group)					
Some college	.060	.065	.151	.158	.160
Bachelor's degree	.187	.447	.498	.442	.469
Postgraduate degree	.136	.554	.606	.631	.667

SOURCE: 1996–1999 CPS ORG data.

NOTE: The reported figures are estimated coefficients on indicators of schooling level from ordinary least squares regressions in which the dependent variable is the natural logarithm of average hourly earnings. These regressions also control for survey month/year, geographic location, and age.

obtained their diploma by passing an equivalency exam.[10] The coefficients on this GED indicator, reported in Table 3.11, represent the approximate percentage wage differential between GED recipients and other high school graduates. In this table, standard errors of the estimated coefficients are shown in parentheses.

Among U.S.-born workers, Table 3.11 indicates that GED recipients earn wages similar to or less than those earned by people who completed

---

[10]Note that the "high school graduate" education category includes only individuals who completed high school but did not go on to take any college classes. Unfortunately, even the 1998 and 1999 CPS do not identify the GED status of those who pursued postsecondary education.

Table 3.11

Returns to a GED, by Race/Ethnicity and Generation, Ages 25–59, U.S. Total

Race/Ethnicity/Generation	Men	Women
Mexican Americans		
Immigrant	.088	.159
	(.049)	(.065)
2nd generation	.013	.021
	(.058)	(.069)
3rd+ generation	−.153	−.020
	(.039)	(.040)
3rd+ generation whites	−.073	−.103
	(.009)	(.010)
3rd+ generation blacks	−.061	−.051
	(.025)	(.023)

SOURCE: 1998–1999 CPS ORG data.

NOTE: Standard errors are shown in parentheses. The reported figures are estimated coefficients on a GED indicator from ordinary least squares regressions in which the dependent variable is the natural logarithm of average hourly earnings. They represent the log wage differential between GED recipients and other high school graduates. These regressions also control for survey month/year, geographic location, age, and education level.

high school the traditional way. In particular, for second-generation Mexican Americans and for third-generation Mexican American women, GED recipients earn about the same wages as other high school graduates, whereas for whites, blacks, and third-generation Mexican American men, GED recipients earn less than workers with conventional high school diplomas. Among Mexican immigrants, however, GED recipients earn substantially *more* than other high school graduates, with GED wage advantages of 9 percent for men and 16 percent for women.

For two reasons, these results should be interpreted with caution. First, as evident from the standard errors in Table 3.11, the estimated coefficients are imprecise for all groups except whites, because of the relatively small samples of GED recipients (roughly one-third of workers fall into the "high school graduate" education category, and only about

11 percent of these individuals have a GED).[11] Second, studies with more detailed information about workers' backgrounds and characteristics find that for most workers, the GED does not significantly raise earnings above what they would receive as high school dropouts (Cameron and Heckman, 1993; Murnane, Willett, and Tyler, 2000).

Nevertheless, our results suggest that the GED may benefit immigrants in ways not relevant for U.S.-born workers. In particular, the GED might provide a mechanism through which immigrants can certify their educational qualifications for U.S. employers who do not know how to evaluate credentials earned in Mexico or other foreign countries. Analyzing recent CPS data as we do, Clark and Jaeger (2000) find that the wage advantage for GED recipients over other high school graduates remains strong when foreign-born workers from *all* countries are considered, rather than just those from Mexico. In a similar vein, Bratsberg and Ragan (2002) show that immigrants, by acquiring some schooling in the United States, can raise the economic return to the pre-migration education they received in the home country.

Age, as a proxy for work experience, is another key determinant of worker earnings. Tables 3.12 to 3.15 report the age coefficients from the regressions that underlie Tables 3.7 to 3.10. These coefficients represent the approximate percentage wage growth that workers experience between the ages of 25 and 29 and the indicated age interval. Mexican immigrants exhibit relatively modest wage differences across age groups, with gaps between the highest-paid and lowest-paid groups of only 10 percent. U.S.-born workers, by contrast, display much more substantial earnings growth with age. To some extent, this pattern signals the low value that U.S. employers place on the work experience that immigrants acquire in Mexico before they come to this country (Chiswick, 1978). In addition, many Mexican immigrants work in unskilled jobs with limited opportunities for career wage growth (Bean and Tienda, 1987; Schoeni, 1997).

Among those born in the United States, age-earnings profiles have a flatter trajectory for women than for men, which at least in part reflects

---

[11]Because of the relatively small samples of GED recipients, we report estimates only for the United States as a whole.

Table 3.12

Returns to Age, by Race/Ethnicity and Generation, Ages 25–59, U.S. Total

| Age Group | | Mexican Americans | | 3rd Generation Whites | 3rd Generation Blacks |
	Immigrant	2nd Generation	3rd+ Generation		
Men					
25–29 (reference group)					
30–34	.036	.136	.061	.144	.073
35–39	.058	.214	.178	.268	.135
40–44	.090	.257	.239	.307	.176
45–49	.095	.270	.231	.315	.248
50–54	.098	.241	.247	.337	.277
55–59	−.003	.289	.258	.332	.252
Women					
25–29 (reference group)					
30–34	.008	.059	.046	.106	.065
35–39	.035	.111	.105	.166	.140
40–44	.009	.227	.155	.183	.176
45–49	.032	.126	.140	.185	.212
50–54	−.022	.187	.183	.188	.236
55–59	.085	.176	.112	.153	.196

SOURCE: 1996–1999 CPS ORG data.

NOTE: The reported figures are estimated coefficients on age-group indicators from ordinary least squares regressions in which the dependent variable is the natural logarithm of average hourly earnings. These regressions also control for survey month/year, geographic location, and education level.

the greater tendency for women to interrupt or adjust their careers for family and other reasons. Wages grow with age at about the same rate for U.S.-born workers of different races and ethnicities, with a couple of exceptions. Among men, earnings growth is higher for whites than for minorities (for example, wage growth between the age intervals of 25–29 and 50–54 is 24 percent for second-generation Mexican Americans, 25 percent for third-generation Mexican Americans, 28 percent for blacks, and 34 percent for whites). Among women, blacks display the highest growth (wage gains between the age intervals of 25–29 and 50–54 of 24 percent, compared to 18 to 19 percent for U.S.-born Mexican Americans and whites). In general, the patterns of age effects just described for the

Table 3.13

Returns to Age, by Race/Ethnicity and Generation, Ages 25–59, California

		Mexican Americans		3rd	3rd
		2nd	3rd+	Generation	Generation
Age Group	Immigrant	Generation	Generation	Whites	Blacks
		Men			
25–29 (reference group)					
30–34	.037	.195	.139	.132	.072
35–39	.098	.312	.189	.283	.145
40–44	.137	.283	.353	.350	.333
45–49	.110	.203	.352	.329	.243
50–54	.152	.302	.274	.309	.331
55–59	−.043	.242	.227	.394	.251
		Women			
25–29 (reference group)					
30–34	.010	.034	.066	.115	.098
35–39	.078	.196	.072	.180	.214
40–44	.044	.237	.118	.209	.198
45–49	.045	.133	.112	.233	.231
50–54	−.021	.321	.148	.228	.229
55–59	.172	.265	.029	.179	.224

SOURCE: 1996–1999 CPS ORG data.

NOTE: The reported figures are estimated coefficients on age-group indicators from ordinary least squares regressions in which the dependent variable is the natural logarithm of average hourly earnings. These regressions also control for survey month/year, geographic location, and education level.

United States as a whole (Table 3.12) also emerge within regions (Tables 3.13 to 3.15).

Wage Decompositions

Well-known statistical techniques exist for decomposing the wage differential between two groups of workers into components attributable to differences in average characteristics of the groups and components attributable to intergroup differences in labor market returns to these characteristics (Oaxaca and Ransom, 1994). This type of decomposition analysis provides a useful way of tying together the discussions of wage comparisons and wage determinants in the preceding two sections.

Table 3.14

Returns to Age, by Race/Ethnicity and Generation, Ages 25–59, Texas

Age Group	Mexican Americans			3rd Generation Whites	3rd Generation Blacks
	Immigrant	2nd Generation	3rd+ Generation		
Men					
25–29 (reference group)					
30–34	.031	.053	.050	.136	.012
35–39	−.0002	.109	.165	.265	.101
40–44	−.024	.235	.180	.271	.142
45–49	−.014	.330	.186	.291	.234
50–54	−.010	.130	.220	.308	.217
55–59	.016	.228	.219	.284	.238
Women					
25–29 (reference group)					
30–34	.010	.046	.015	.070	.067
35–39	.0001	.064	.067	.162	.155
40–44	.024	.213	.110	.156	.190
45–49	.010	.075	.089	.140	.181
50–54	−.054	.065	.141	.125	.318
55–59	−.054	.110	.054	.129	.167

SOURCE: 1996–1999 CPS ORG data.

NOTE: The reported figures are estimated coefficients on age-group indicators from ordinary least squares regressions in which the dependent variable is the natural logarithm of average hourly earnings. These regressions also control for survey month/year, geographic location, and education level.

In the current context, the wage decompositions reveal the extent to which minority wage deficits (relative to white workers) can be explained by lower stocks of the crude human capital measures—education and age—available in CPS data. The remaining portions of the wage deficits are attributed to minorities being paid less than whites for the same observable skills. We perform these decompositions using the regressions that underlie Tables 3.7 to 3.10 and 3.12 to 3.15. Differences between groups in labor market skills and other relevant characteristics (such as geographic location) are represented by differences in the average values of the explanatory variables in these regressions. Differences between

Table 3.15

Returns to Age, by Race/Ethnicity and Generation, Ages 25–59, United States Excluding California and Texas

	Mexican Americans			3rd Generation Whites	3rd Generation Blacks
Age Group	Immigrant	2nd Generation	3rd+ Generation		
		Men			
25–29 (reference group)					
30–34	.041	.133	.033	.145	.080
35–39	.039	.188	.223	.267	.138
40–44	.100	.264	.226	.305	.167
45–49	.138	.253	.205	.314	.250
50–54	.097	.258	.322	.341	.277
55–59	.027	.387	.309	.328	.254
		Women			
25–29 (reference group)					
30–34	.015	.091	.088	.107	.062
35–39	−.006	−.005	.178	.164	.134
40–44	−.043	.191	.241	.181	.172
45–49	.063	.173	.225	.183	.212
50–54	−.006	.077	.316	.187	.230
55–59	.091	.095	.315	.150	.196

SOURCE: 1996–1999 CPS ORG data.

NOTE: The reported figures are estimated coefficients on age-group indicators from ordinary least squares regressions in which the dependent variable is the natural logarithm of average hourly earnings. These regressions also control for survey month/year, geographic location, and education level.

groups in the economic returns to skills are represented by differences in the estimated regression coefficients, including the intercepts.

Given the coarseness of the skill measures employed, we view the resulting decompositions as providing conservative estimates of the importance of human capital differences in explaining minority-white wage gaps. For example, the CPS supplies information about the quantity but not the quality of education. Therefore, if whites attend better schools than minorities on average, our regressions will indicate higher returns to education for whites, when in fact the true returns to schooling of a given quality may be the same for whites and minorities. In the wage decompositions, school quality and other unobserved skill differences between groups could show up in the portion of the wage gap attributed to differing labor market returns, even if they really belong in the portion of the wage gap arising from human capital differences. To take another example, English language proficiency is an important determinant of earnings for Mexican Americans, but the CPS data we analyze do not provide useful language information. Although this omission most directly affects the estimates for Mexican immigrants, the effect is not limited to immigrants, because significant fractions of second- and third-generation Mexican Americans lack complete fluency in English (Trejo, 1997). By failing to incorporate language skills, the wage decompositions reported below are likely to understate the portion of Mexican-white wage gaps resulting from human capital differences.

Table 3.16 presents the wage decompositions that pertain to the entire United States for men ages 25–59. The last row of the table shows the total log wage differentials between third-generation whites and each of the minority groups. These total differentials are simply the differences in average log wages between whites and minorities, without adjusting for worker characteristics. The remaining rows break down the total differentials into components representing the effect of mean differences in particular characteristics and the effect of differences in the estimated returns to these characteristics.[12] Decompositions such as these can be normalized in various ways. The decompositions reported in the columns labeled (1) use the white coefficients to weight the differences in average characteristics and the minority group's average characteristics to weight the differences in coefficients. Alternatively, the decompositions reported in the columns labeled (2) use the minority group's coefficients to weight the differences in average characteristics and the white characteristics to weight the differences in coefficients.

---

[12]The portion of a wage gap attributed to minority-white differences in the returns to any *particular* variable depends on typically arbitrary decisions about how this variable is normalized (Oaxaca and Ransom, 1999). For this reason, we report only the overall share of the wage gap that is due to differing returns (versus differing characteristics), as well as the portion of the wage gap attributable to mean differences in particular characteristics. The quantities that we report are not sensitive to how the variables are normalized.

Table 3.16

Decomposition of Log Hourly Wage Differentials Relative to 3rd+ Generation Whites, Men Ages 25–59, U.S. Total

	Mexican Americans								3rd Generation Blacks	
	Recent Immigrant		Earlier Immigrant		2nd Generation		3rd Generation			
	(1)	(2)	(1)	(2)	(1)	(2)	(1)	(2)	(1)	(2)
Percentage of wage differential attributable to differences in average characteristics										
Education	42.8	31.0	61.1	44.3	47.7	55.1	46.1	45.9	23.1	22.8
Age	14.7	3.4	2.2	0.4	15.3	12.1	9.3	7.6	3.9	3.6
Other	-4.5	-4.5	-7.3	-7.3	-6.6	-6.6	-2.1	-2.1	3.1	3.1
Subtotal	53.0	29.9	56.0	37.4	56.4	60.6	53.3	51.5	30.2	29.6
Percentage of wage differential attributable to differences in coefficients	47.0	70.1	44.0	62.6	43.6	39.4	46.7	48.5	69.8	70.4
Total log wage differential	0.705		0.503		0.238		0.242		0.299	

SOURCE: 1996–1999 CPS ORG data.

NOTE: The column (1) decompositions use the white coefficients to weight the differences in average characteristics and the minority group's average characteristics to weight the differences in coefficients. The column (2) decompositions use the minority group's coefficients to weight the differences in average characteristics and the white characteristics to weight the differences in coefficients.

The alternative decompositions generally yield similar results, except, as discussed below, for Mexican immigrants.

Table 3.16 reveals striking differences between U.S.-born Mexican American and black men in the portion of their respective hourly wage deficits (relative to whites) that can be attributed to observable skill differences. Overall, second- and third-generation Mexican Americans earn wages 24 percent below those of whites. The decompositions indicate that the majority (52 to 61 percent) of this wage gap is explained by racial/ethnic differences in the average characteristics of workers. By itself, the lower educational attainment of Mexican Americans accounts for about half (46 to 55 percent) of their wage deficit, and the relative youth of this population explains a smaller portion (8 to 15 percent). The "other" variables included in the regressions are indicators for geographic location and survey month/year.[13] Rather than helping to explain the Mexican wage deficit, racial/ethnic differences in these other variables actually make the unadjusted wage gap a bit smaller than it would be otherwise, primarily because Mexican Americans are heavily concentrated in California, a state with relatively high wages and costs of living.

By contrast, skill differences account for only 30 percent of the black-white male wage gap. As with Mexican Americans, education is the key factor, but the share of the wage deficit attributable to education differences is half as large for blacks (23 percent) as for Mexican Americans. Not only do observable skills explain more of the wage gap for Mexican Americans than for blacks, but the wage deficit to be explained is smaller for Mexican Americans (24 percent) than it is for blacks (30 percent). These findings echo previous studies (Reimers, 1983; Darity, Guilkey, and Winfrey, 1995; Trejo, 1997) which suggest that, among U.S.-born men, the wage structure and labor market opportunities are much more similar for Mexican Americans and whites

---

[13]Because the coefficients of the geographic and survey month/year variables are restricted to be the same across ethnic groups, these variables contribute only to the portion of the wage gap attributable to differences in characteristics. In addition, the magnitude of this contribution does not depend on how the decompositions are normalized, resulting in column (1) and column (2) estimates that are identical for this set of variables.

than they are for blacks and whites. To a large extent, Mexican American men earn low wages because they possess less human capital than other men.

Less education also explains much of the wage deficit for Mexican immigrant men, but here the magnitude of the explained portion is sensitive to how the decompositions are normalized. In the columns labeled (1), where the estimated returns to education for third-generation whites are used to value the differences in average schooling levels, these education differences explain 43 percent of the wage gap for recent immigrants and 61 percent of the wage gap for earlier immigrants. In the columns labeled (2), however, smaller portions of the wage gap are attributed to education differences (31 percent for recent immigrants and 44 percent for earlier immigrants), because these alternative decompositions value schooling differences using immigrant returns to education, which are much lower than those of U.S.-born workers.

In Tables 3.17 to 3.19, the same patterns show up when the wage decompositions are performed separately by region of the country. The contrast between Mexican American and black men in the underlying sources of wage disadvantage is even sharper in California than elsewhere. In the golden state, education and age account for 60 to 77 percent of the wage gap (relative to whites) for second- and third-generation Mexican Americans, whereas these same factors explain less than one-quarter of the black-white wage gap.

Tables 3.20 to 3.23 present analogous wage decompositions for women. Unadjusted wage deficits are larger for U.S.-born Mexican Americans than for blacks, especially in California (total wage gaps exceeding 20 percent for Mexican Americans versus 13 percent for blacks) and Texas (total wage gaps of about 30 percent for Mexican Americans versus 18 percent for blacks). This pattern for women is opposite that observed for men, except in Texas. Nevertheless, the other patterns for women are similar to those described above for men. Racial/ethnic differences in educational attainment are a primary determinant of male wage gaps, and they play an even larger role for women. For the United States as a whole (Table 3.20), schooling differences explain 64 to 76 percent of the wage deficit for second- and third-generation Mexican American women (compared to 46 to 55

Table 3.17

Decomposition of Log Hourly Wage Differentials Relative to 3rd+ Generation Whites, Men Ages 25–59, California

| | Mexican Americans | | | | | | | | 3rd Generation Blacks | |
| | Recent Immigrant | | Earlier Immigrant | | 2nd Generation | | 3rd Generation | | | |
	(1)	(2)	(1)	(2)	(1)	(2)	(1)	(2)	(1)	(2)
Percentage of wage differential attributable to differences in average characteristics										
Education	45.8	33.6	60.6	44.6	55.5	61.9	54.6	53.5	17.0	20.0
Age	14.4	4.5	2.4	0.2	21.5	14.2	8.4	6.3	4.8	4.6
Other	−0.4	−0.4	0.1	0.1	1.0	1.0	−0.5	−0.5	0.8	0.8
Subtotal	59.8	37.7	63.0	44.9	77.9	77.2	62.5	59.3	22.6	25.4
Percentage of wage differential attributable to differences in coefficients	40.2	62.3	37.0	55.1	22.1	22.8	37.5	40.7	77.4	74.6
Total log wage differential	0.859		0.640		0.265		0.268		0.303	

SOURCE: 1996–1999 CPS ORG data.

NOTE: The column (1) decompositions use the white coefficients to weight the differences in average characteristics and the minority group's average characteristics to weight the differences in coefficients. The column (2) decompositions use the minority group's coefficients to weight the differences in average characteristics and the white characteristics to weight the differences in coefficients.

Table 3.18

Decomposition of Log Hourly Wage Differentials Relative to 3rd+ Generation Whites, Men Ages 25–59, Texas

| | Mexican Americans | | | | | | | | 3rd Generation Blacks | |
| | Recent Immigrant | | Earlier Immigrant | | 2nd Generation | | 3rd Generation | | | |
	(1)	(2)	(1)	(2)	(1)	(2)	(1)	(2)	(1)	(2)
Percentage of wage differential attributable to differences in average characteristics										
Education	44.6	28.1	61.1	39.3	46.4	52.7	48.8	45.9	24.5	23.1
Age	10.5	–0.9	1.0	–0.5	5.3	4.4	5.7	4.8	6.7	6.3
Other	–0.3	–0.3	–0.4	–0.4	2.4	2.4	–1.1	–1.1	–1.0	–1.0
Subtotal	54.7	26.9	61.8	38.4	54.1	59.5	53.5	49.7	30.2	28.3
Percentage of wage differential attributable to differences in coefficients	45.3	73.1	38.2	61.6	45.9	40.5	46.5	50.3	69.8	71.7
Total log wage differential	0.727		0.570		0.399		0.367		0.311	

SOURCE: 1996–1999 CPS ORG data.

NOTE: The column (1) decompositions use the white coefficients to weight the differences in average characteristics and the minority group's average characteristics to weight the differences in coefficients. The column (2) decompositions use the minority group's coefficients to weight the differences in average characteristics and the white characteristics to weight the differences in coefficients.

Table 3.19

Decomposition of Log Hourly Wage Differentials Relative to 3rd+ Generation Whites, Men Ages 25–59, United States Excluding California and Texas

| | Mexican Americans | | | | | | | | 3rd Generation Blacks | |
| | Recent Immigrant | | Earlier Immigrant | | 2nd Generation | | 3rd Generation | | | |
	(1)	(2)	(1)	(2)	(1)	(2)	(1)	(2)	(1)	(2)
Percentage of wage differential attributable to differences in average characteristics										
Education	42.8	26.8	63.5	40.0	44.9	42.9	48.2	40.5	23.5	23.4
Age	15.0	4.4	3.0	1.0	14.3	11.0	13.1	13.0	3.5	3.3
Other	−0.8	−0.8	0.9	0.9	5.9	5.9	6.1	6.1	3.9	3.9
Subtotal	56.9	30.4	67.4	41.9	65.1	59.8	67.4	59.7	31.0	30.7
Percentage of wage differential attributable to differences in coefficients	43.1	69.6	32.6	58.1	34.9	40.2	32.6	40.3	69.0	69.3
Total log wage differential	0.684		0.478		0.232		0.175		0.297	

SOURCE: 1996–1999 CPS ORG data.

NOTE: The column (1) decompositions use the white coefficients to weight the differences in average characteristics and the minority group's average characteristics to weight the differences in coefficients. The column (2) decompositions use the minority group's coefficients to weight the differences in average characteristics and the white characteristics to weight the differences in coefficients.

Table 3.20

Decomposition of Log Hourly Wage Differentials Relative to 3rd+ Generation Whites, Women Ages 25–59, U.S. Total

| | Mexican Americans | | | | | | | | 3rd Generation Blacks | |
| | Recent Immigrant | | Earlier Immigrant | | 2nd Generation | | 3rd Generation | | | |
	(1)	(2)	(1)	(2)	(1)	(2)	(1)	(2)	(1)	(2)
Percentage of wage differential attributable to differences in average characteristics										
Education	59.7	44.3	73.8	55.4	72.8	70.6	64.3	75.7	40.7	43.1
Age	6.5	1.0	0.5	0.0	12.6	12.3	3.8	4.7	3.2	5.8
Other	−11.9	−11.9	−14.9	−14.9	−29.6	−29.6	−7.9	−7.9	−4.5	−4.5
Subtotal	54.3	33.5	59.4	40.5	55.8	53.4	60.2	72.5	39.4	44.4
Percentage of wage differential attributable to differences in coefficients	45.7	66.5	40.6	59.5	44.2	46.6	39.8	27.5	60.6	55.6
Total log wage differential	0.600		0.455		0.160		0.193		0.150	

SOURCE: 1996–1999 CPS ORG data.

NOTE: The column (1) decompositions use the white coefficients to weight the differences in average characteristics and the minority group's average characteristics to weight the differences in coefficients. The column (2) decompositions use the minority group's coefficients to weight the differences in average characteristics and the white characteristics to weight the differences in coefficients.

Table 3.21

Decomposition of Log Hourly Wage Differentials Relative to 3rd+ Generation Whites, Women Ages 25–59, California

| | Mexican Americans | | | | | | | | 3rd Generation Blacks | |
| | Recent Immigrant | | Earlier Immigrant | | 2nd Generation | | 3rd Generation | | | |
	(1)	(2)	(1)	(2)	(1)	(2)	(1)	(2)	(1)	(2)
Percentage of wage differential attributable to differences in average characteristics										
Education	65.9	49.5	76.8	59.3	63.2	53.7	70.0	75.4	23.1	25.9
Age	6.4	1.8	0.8	-0.1	11.1	12.1	4.1	2.1	2.3	3.5
Other	-0.6	-0.6	-0.4	-0.4	-0.4	-0.4	-2.5	-2.5	-2.7	-2.7
Subtotal	71.8	50.8	77.2	58.9	73.9	65.4	71.5	74.9	22.8	26.8
Percentage of wage differential attributable to differences in coefficients	28.2	49.2	22.8	41.1	26.1	34.6	28.5	25.1	77.2	73.2
Total log wage differential	0.795		0.610		0.257		0.211		0.131	

SOURCE: 1996–1999 CPS ORG data.

NOTE: The column (1) decompositions use the white coefficients to weight the differences in average characteristics and the minority group's average characteristics to weight the differences in coefficients. The column (2) decompositions use the minority group's coefficients to weight the differences in average characteristics and the white characteristics to weight the differences in coefficients.

Table 3.22

Decomposition of Log Hourly Wage Differentials Relative to 3rd+ Generation Whites, Women Ages 25–59, Texas

| | Mexican Americans | | | | | | | | 3rd Generation Blacks | |
| | Recent Immigrant | | Earlier Immigrant | | 2nd Generation | | 3rd Generation | | | |
	(1)	(2)	(1)	(2)	(1)	(2)	(1)	(2)	(1)	(2)
Percentage of wage differential attributable to differences in average characteristics										
Education	45.3	40.5	53.4	48.6	48.9	54.3	50.3	61.3	38.2	42.4
Age	3.2	-1.0	0.0	0.0	6.0	4.9	1.8	1.9	5.0	10.9
Other	-2.6	-2.6	-0.1	-0.1	0.9	0.9	-0.3	-0.3	-0.8	-0.8
Subtotal	45.9	36.9	53.3	48.5	55.9	60.1	51.8	63.0	42.4	52.5
Percentage of wage differential attributable to differences in coefficients	54.1	63.1	46.7	51.5	44.1	39.9	48.2	37.0	57.6	47.5
Total log wage differential	0.680		0.570		0.290		0.320		0.177	

SOURCE: 1996–1999 CPS ORG data.

NOTE: The column (1) decompositions use the white coefficients to weight the differences in average characteristics and the minority group's average characteristics to weight the differences in coefficients. The column (2) decompositions use the minority group's coefficients to weight the differences in average characteristics and the white characteristics to weight the differences in coefficients.

Table 3.23

Decomposition of Log Hourly Wage Differentials Relative to 3rd+ Generation Whites, Women Ages 25–59, United States Excluding California and Texas

| | Mexican Americans | | | | | | | | 3rd Generation Blacks | |
| | Recent Immigrant | | Earlier Immigrant | | 2nd Generation | | 3rd Generation | | | |
	(1)	(2)	(1)	(2)	(1)	(2)	(1)	(2)	(1)	(2)
Percentage of wage differential attributable to differences in average characteristics										
Education	61.6	26.3	78.1	33.2	72.9	73.2	72.0	78.3	42.6	44.8
Age	7.6	1.1	0.9	1.2	9.9	9.2	6.1	15.3	2.9	5.6
Other	-3.6	-3.6	0.1	0.1	-0.4	-0.4	7.7	7.7	-4.7	-4.7
Subtotal	65.7	23.8	79.1	34.6	82.4	82.0	85.9	101.3	40.8	45.7
Percentage of wage differential attributable to differences in coefficients	34.3	76.2	20.9	65.4	17.6	18.0	14.1	-1.3	59.2	54.3
Total log wage differential	0.540		0.409		0.142		0.142		0.146	

SOURCE: 1996–1999 CPS ORG data.

NOTE: The column (1) decompositions use the white coefficients to weight the differences in average characteristics and the minority group's average characteristics to weight the differences in coefficients. The column (2) decompositions use the minority group's coefficients to weight the differences in average characteristics and the white characteristics to weight the differences in coefficients.

percent for men in Table 3.16) and 41 to 43 percent of the wage deficit for black women (compared to 23 percent for men). For Mexican immigrants as well, education differences account for a bigger percentage of the female wage gap than of the male wage gap. Finally, as was the case for men, observable skills explain a much larger portion of the wage gap for Mexican American women than for black women, more so in California than in Texas.

4. Determinants of High School Graduation

In the previous two chapters, we saw that men and women of Mexican descent acquire much less schooling than other groups in the United States and that this educational deficit is an important cause of the relatively low earnings of Mexican-origin workers. Thus, a key economic problem confronting Mexican Americans is insufficient schooling. In this chapter, we try to better understand this important problem by examining in detail the determinants of racial/ethnic differences in an important educational outcome: high school graduation.

The analysis in Chapter 2 showed that there were two dimensions of the educational problem facing Mexican Americans. First, recent immigrants on average have markedly low attainment levels. Second, although the second generation gains substantial ground, important gaps remain between their educational attainment and that of U.S. whites.

Since the attainment levels of new immigrants fall largely beyond the realm of the U.S. education system, we focus in this chapter on U.S.-born Mexican Americans. We also include in our analysis children who arrive in this country before they are five years old. This group of "near-natives" receives much of its schooling in the United States and graduates at about the same rate as U.S.-born Mexican Americans.[1]

We use data from the NELS to analyze the remaining graduation gap in more detail. We first consider the roles of family structure, parental education, and family income. Prior research has shown these factors to be important determinants of educational attainment.

---

[1]Appendix B provides a detailed comparison of graduation rates in the CPS and the National Education Longitudinal Survey.

We then attempt to shed some light on the reasons why parental education and family income affect students' high school graduation rates and racial/ethnic graduation differentials. To do this, we construct a number of measures from the NELS that may indicate ways that parents influence the educational environment facing their children. If more-educated parents do more to encourage literacy, for example, and literacy, in turn, increases schooling, then literacy-enhancing activities on the part of the parent may "explain" the effect of parental education on their children's graduation rates. If literacy promotion varies by race/ethnicity, it may help explain the role of parental education on racial/ethnic graduation differentials as well.

Finally, we consider the role of schools in understanding the link between family background, high school graduation, and racial and ethnic graduation gaps. Family income, in particular, may influence where a family sends its children to school. To the extent that black and Mexican American families have lower income than whites, family income could explain graduation differentials by explaining the quality of schools that students of different races and ethnicities attend. Since meaningful measures of school quality are difficult to construct from readily observed differences in school resources (Betts, 1996), we do not estimate the effects of school quality, but rather employ a methodology that allows us to ask about the effects of family background on high school graduation rates and racial/ethnic graduation differentials, holding school quality constant.

Data

Some Background on the NELS

Most of our analysis is based on data from the NELS, which began in the spring of 1988 with a clustered national probability sample of students attending the eighth grade. The sample design ensured that an average of roughly 24 students was included from each sampled school. Most of these students were then interviewed again in 1990, 1992, and 1994. The 1994 survey can be used to construct a high school *graduation* measure, which is equal to 1 if the student received a diploma within roughly two years of his normal graduation date. It can also be used to construct a high school *completion* measure which equals 1 for both high school graduates and GED recipients. We limit our analysis here to the graduation measure.

In the 1988 survey, the NELS collected a number of family structure measures, including the presence of the father in the household and the number of children in the family. It also collected data on the parents' educational attainment and family income, both of which are known to have important effects on high school graduation and racial/ethnic graduation differentials (Cameron and Heckman, 2001). Because these crucial data items are missing for most of the NELS students who did not participate in the 1988 survey, we exclude such students from the analysis.

The 1988 NELS survey also provides measures of parental and student behavior that may indicate parents' attempts to influence the educational attainment of their children. Some of these measures are constructed from student questionnaire items, although some are constructed from a parent questionnaire that was fielded in 1988.[2] As we explain in more detail below, these items include measures of language use, literacy-related activities and consumption patterns, familial communication regarding school matters, after-school child care arrangements, and some general social capital measures. In some cases, similar measures can be constructed from both student and parent questionnaire items.

We cannot necessarily determine the causal effects of these parental influence measures. In some cases, such as rules regarding homework or television, issues of reverse causation may arise: Rules imposed by the parents may be a response to poor performance by the student rather than a cause of good performance. More generally, it is unclear whether these behaviors are the true causes of students' educational attainment or whether they are merely correlated with unobservables which themselves are the true causes of both the student's attainment and our observable behavior measures.

---

[2] Because of the importance of the parent questionnaire to our approach, we exclude from the sample students whose parents did not complete the 1988 parent survey. This amounts to a minor restriction, since over 92 percent of the base year students' parents completed the parent survey.

Of course, the same can be said of parental education and family income. Indeed, our desire to understand how those measures affect educational attainment and racial/ethnic attainment differentials leads us to include the parental influence measures in our models. These measures may help illuminate the mechanisms by which parental education and income influence the student's education, even if our measures are not the true causal factors that are responsible for the link between family background and the student's educational attainment.

Although the measures of family background and parental behavior represent an important advantage of the NELS for studying graduation rates and graduation rate differentials, the NELS does have an important disadvantage as well. Because its sample size is relatively small, it is impossible to provide state-specific regression analyses, as we did in Chapters 2 and 3. All of the results presented here are for the United States as a whole.

High School Graduation and Family Background

Table 4.1 summarizes the high school graduation and family background measures that appear in the regression analysis. Column (1) presents overall sample means whereas columns (2) through (4) present means by race and ethnicity. The dependent variable for the regression analysis is a high school graduation dummy that equals 1 if the student graduated with a diploma and equals 0 otherwise.[3] Students of Mexican heritage have nearly the same graduation rate as blacks, which is about 12 percentage points below the 85.6 percent graduation rate of whites.

The gap between whites and Mexican Americans is smaller in the NELS than in the CPS. As we show in Appendix B, part of the reason for this difference is simply that the NELS shows smaller graduation differentials for all minority groups, suggesting that it misses some of the most disadvantaged students. The other reason has to do with the difference between graduating high school with a diploma and completing high school by either graduating or obtaining a GED. For

---

[3]In other words, we exclude GED recipients from our definition of high school graduates.

Table 4.1

Means of Family Characteristics, by Race and Ethnicity

Variable	Total (1)	Whites (2)	Blacks (3)	Mexican Americans (4)
High school graduate (%)	83.0	85.6	73.1	73.4
Near-native (%)	1.8	1.0	1.7	11.8
Black (%)	13.5	—	100	—
Mexican American (%)	6.8	—	—	100
Female (%)	50.0	49.9	49.9	51.4
Number of siblings	2.26	2.14	2.64	2.98
Father absent (%)	30.6	26.2	58.3	28.2
Mother born in United States (%)	92.8	95.8	93.1	56.7
Father born in United States (%)	92.6	96.0	92.5	52.9
Mother's education (%)				
Less than high school	14.7	11.9	15.6	46.6
High school	20.9	24.6	18.7	14.8
Some college	38.2	38.9	40.6	26.0
College degree	15.4	17.3	10.4	3.0
Family income (%)				
< $10,000	10.8	7.0	27.4	22.8
$10,000–$15,000	8.0	6.2	14.2	16.2
$15,000–$20,000	6.8	6.1	8.7	11.5
$20,000–$25,000	10.2	9.9	11.4	11.7
$25,000–$35,000	18.1	18.8	14.7	16.3
> $35,000	42.2	48.1	20.1	18.5
Sample size	11,183	8,765	1,325	1,093

NOTE: Based on weighted data. Maternal education and family income categories do not sum to 1 because of the presence of missing values.

U.S.-born students in the NELS, whites have completion rates of 90.6 percent, compared to 83.0 percent for blacks and 79.6 percent for Mexican Americans. Completion rates for near-natives are similar.

The next row of the table shows that there are very few near natives among the white and black students, compared to about 12 percent among Mexican Americans. Moving down the table a bit, we see that Mexican Americans have somewhat larger families than blacks, who in turn have larger families than whites. In the context of a quality-quantity model of fertility (Becker, 1981), one would expect parents in small families to invest more in each child than parents in large families. In that case, the family-size differences observed here would lead whites to have the highest graduation rates and Mexican Americans to have the lowest graduation rates, all else equal.

Twenty-five to 30 percent of white and Mexican American students live apart from their fathers, compared to nearly 60 percent of blacks. Very few whites and blacks have parents who were born abroad, whereas nearly half of the Mexican American students have at least one parent who was born outside the United States. Maternal education distributions differ by race and ethnicity as well. Black students are somewhat more likely than whites to have a mother who dropped out of high school and a bit less likely to have a mother who graduated from college. However, nearly half of the Mexican American students had mothers who did not finish high school, a rate three to four times higher than the corresponding rates for blacks and whites. Family incomes vary, too, although the major differences here are between whites on the one hand and blacks and Mexican Americans on the other. Whereas only 7 percent of white families have incomes less than $10,000, 27 percent of blacks and 23 percent of Mexican American families fall into this lowest income category.[4]

Regression Results

The Importance of Family Background

If these family characteristics explain high school graduation, then the fact that they differ so much by race/ethnicity suggests that they may explain racial and ethnic graduation differentials as well. The first column of Table 4.2 reports the results from a regression of the high school graduation dummy on the family characteristics just discussed. Controlling for family characteristics reduces the white-minority graduation gaps by a great deal. The black dummy has a coefficient (standard error) of only −0.020 (0.029), compared to the unconditional graduation differential of 0.125 from Table 4.1. The coefficient on the Mexican American dummy is quite similar, at −0.027 (0.023). This compares to an unconditional differential of 0.122. For both groups,

---

[4]The NELS provides four categories for incomes above $35,000. We collapsed them into a single "over $35,000" category because preliminary analyses showed their effects on high school graduation to be similar.

56

Table 4.2

High School Graduation Regressions, by Race/Ethnicity

	Total (1)	White (2)	Black (3)	Mexican American (4)
Near-native	−0.006	−0.025	0.040	0.020
	(0.037)	(0.037)	(0.159)	(0.053)
Black	−0.020			
	(0.029)			
Mexican American	−0.027			
	(0.023)			
Female	0.030	0.020	0.074	0.003
	(0.012)	(0.011)	(0.043)	(0.035)
Number of siblings	−0.010	−0.012	−0.003	−0.033
	(0.004)	(0.004)	(0.012)	(0.012)
Father absent	−0.087	−0.078	−0.130	−0.079
	(0.018)	(0.019)	(0.054)	(0.049)
Mother born in United States	−0.019	0.017	−0.051	−0.037
	(0.035)	(0.034)	(0.118)	(0.061)
Father born in United States	−0.046	−0.050	−0.026	−0.072
	(0.028)	(0.024)	(0.128)	(0.062)
Mother's education				
Less than high school	−0.143	−0.167	−0.109	0.002
	(0.021)	(0.023)	(0.052)	(0.070)
Some college	0.013	0.014	−0.010	0.075
	(0.012)	(0.013)	(0.037)	(0.063)
College degree	0.051	0.060	−0.021	0.034
	(0.016)	(0.012)	(0.101)	(0.067)
Family income				
< $10,000	−0.186	−0.214	−0.121	−0.344
	(0.034)	(0.035)	(0.078)	(0.058)
$10,000–$15,000	−0.123	−0.121	−0.067	−0.272
	(0.027)	(0.030)	(0.079)	(0.061)
$15,000–$20,000	−0.071	−0.060	−0.092	−0.216
	(0.027)	(0.026)	(0.109)	(0.062)
$20,000–$25,000	−0.066	−0.041	−0.158	−0.176
	(0.022)	(0.020)	(0.092)	(0.067)
$25,000–$35,000	−0.026	−0.010	−0.092	−0.123
	(0.018)	(0.015)	(0.097)	(0.054)
Sample size	11,183	8,765	1,325	1,093
Adjusted R-squared	0.131	0.132	0.105	0.132

NOTE: Based on weighted data. Figures in parentheses are standard errors that have been adjusted for the presence of multiple students/school and for arbitrary forms of heteroskedasticity. To account for these missing values, the regressions include missing value flags in addition to the variables shown. The missing value flag for maternal education equals 1 for all families with missing maternal education data and equals 0 otherwise. The corresponding values of the maternal less-than-high-school, some college, and college degree variables are set to 0. The missing value flag for family income is defined similarly. The regression also includes missing value flags for the number of siblings, father absent, and parental nativity.

family characteristics explain roughly three-quarters of the high school graduation gap.[5]

Inspecting the other coefficients in column (1) makes it easy to see why. The coefficients on family size, family structure, maternal education, and family income are all significant, and these factors all vary substantially by race and ethnicity. Among U.S.-born and near-native students, family characteristics play an important role in explaining both graduation rates and graduation rate differentials.

One potential shortcoming of this simple regression is that it constrains the relationship between family background and high school graduation to be the same for all three racial/ethnic groups. If the true relationship differs, then the constrained regression could yield misleading results. This is particularly important in light of findings by Cameron and Heckman (2001) that similar estimates derived from the National Longitudinal Survey of Youth indeed vary by group.

Columns (2) to (4) present the results from race/ethnicity-specific regressions of the high school graduation dummy on family characteristics. Within this sample of U.S. natives and near-natives, nativity has no effect on graduation rates. White females are slightly (but significantly) more likely to graduate than white males. Gender differences are large for blacks but only marginally significant. There is essentially no gender gap for Mexican Americans. The family size coefficient is significant and of moderate magnitude in the white regression, small and insignificant in the black regression, and significant and substantial in the Mexican American regression. Thus, family size is most important for the group with the largest average family size. As in the pooled regression in column (1), parental nativity is insignificant for all groups.[6]

Substantial racial and ethnic differences emerge in the effects of maternal education. Among whites, students with mothers who were

---

[5]McKinney (1999) reports similar patterns in High School and Beyond data.

[6]Other studies of Hispanic educational attainment report parental nativity to be significant. Our results could differ for two reasons: (1) We restrict the analysis to Hispanics of Mexican heritage, whereas the other studies analyze Hispanics generally; and (2) we limit the analysis to U.S.-born and near-native students of Mexican heritage, whereas the other studies include later immigrants as well.

dropouts or college graduates graduate at significantly different rates than students whose mothers' education ended with high school. For blacks, students whose mothers dropped out are less likely to graduate themselves, but the effect is smaller than that for whites, and children whose mothers went to college do no better on average than children whose mothers' schooling ended with a high school diploma. In contrast, among Mexican American students, the maternal education coefficients are insignificant, both individually and jointly.[7] This is an important finding. On the one hand, it implies that the low levels of education among Mexican American parents may put their children at less of a disadvantage for finishing high school than the descriptive statistics from Table 4.1 suggest. On the other hand, this finding helps to resolve the puzzle noted in Chapter 2, that the huge educational gain between first- and second-generation Mexican Americans is followed by only slight improvement between the second and third generations. According to the estimates in Table 4.2, the intergenerational transmission mechanism expected to produce substantial educational progress between second- and third-generation Mexican Americans is too weak to have much effect.[8]

For whites, low family income is a strong predictor of dropping out. Even controlling for maternal education, students from families with incomes below $10,000 are 21 percentage points less likely to graduate high school than students from families with incomes over $30,000. Even the 4-percentage-point differential among students from families with incomes of $20,000 to $25,000 is significant. In contrast, none of the income coefficients in the black regression is significant, even though all are negative.[9] However, the effects of income are strongest of all for Mexican American students. All of the income coefficients are significant, and all are substantially larger (in absolute value) than the corresponding coefficients in the white regression. Mexican American

---

[7]The F-statistic for the joint test yields a value of 1.12, which has a p-value of 0.34.

[8]This conclusion remains largely unchanged when one adds paternal education to the model.

[9]They are jointly insignificant as well, with an F-statistic of 0.78.

students, whose families generally have low incomes, seem to be most adversely affected by low income.

Within the context of the group-specific regression models, we ask whether family characteristics explain the observed graduation differentials using the Oaxaca decomposition that we used to decompose wage differentials in Chapter 3. Table 4.3 presents results, broken down by components attributable to family background (i.e., gender, family size, family structure, and parental nativity), maternal education, and family income. The fourth row gives the total that can be attributed to differences in mean characteristics by group.

For both blacks and Mexican Americans, family characteristics explain much of the graduation gap. When weighted by the white regression coefficients, differences in mean characteristics explain 89 percent of the white-black gap and 102 percent of the white-Mexican gap. Weighted by the respective minority coefficients, they explain 77 percent of the white-black gap and 79 percent of the white-Mexican gap.

The factors that provide the greatest explanation vary between groups and depend on the coefficients that are used to weight the mean differences in family characteristics. For blacks, both sets of coefficients imply that maternal education differences explain about 2 percentage

Table 4.3

Oaxaca Decomposition of High School Graduation Differentials

	White-Black		White-Mexican American	
	Based on White Coefficients (1)	Based on Black Coefficients (2)	Based on White Coefficients (3)	Based on Mexican American Coefficients (4)
Percentage of Graduation Differential Attributable to Mean Characteristics				
(1) Family background	3.5	4.3	0.3	−0.9
(2) Mother's education	2.1	2.2	7.2	1.3
(3) Family income	5.5	3.1	4.9	9.2
(4) Subtotal	11.1	9.6	12.4	9.6
Percentage of Graduation Differential Attributable to Coefficients				
(5) Subtotal	1.4	2.9	−0.2	2.6
Total graduation differential	12.5	12.5	12.2	12.2

NOTE: Based on regression estimates reported in Table 4.2.

points, or about 17 percent, of the graduation gap between white and black students. Family background and family income play important roles as well, although the exact ranking of these two factors depends on whether one uses the white or black coefficients to do the weighting. Family income appears to explain at least 25 percent of the gap, whereas family background appears to explain at least 28 percent.

For Mexican American students, the explanatory power of the various factors is much more sensitive to the set of coefficients that one uses to weight. Judging by the white coefficients, maternal education by itself explains nearly 60 percent of the graduation gap, and family income explains the remaining 40 percent. According to the Mexican American coefficients, however, family income explains 75 percent whereas maternal education explains only 11 percent.

As a general principle, it is difficult to decide which decomposition is more "correct" when the different sets of coefficients yield substantially different decompositions. In this case, however, an argument can be made for the decomposition based on the Mexican American coefficients. The reason is that the decomposition based on the white coefficients implies that maternal education explains most of the difference in graduation rates, whereas the regression results in Table 4.2 themselves imply clearly that the link between maternal education and the student's own chances of graduating is quite weak for Mexican Americans. This argues for placing greater weight on the decomposition in column (4), which reveals family income, rather than maternal education, to be the primary reason for lower graduation rates among Mexican Americans.

This stands in contrast to the results for blacks. The decompositions in Table 4.3, and the regressions from Table 4.2 on which they are based, show maternal education to be an important factor in explaining the white-black graduation gap. This is consistent with Cameron and Heckman (2001) and Kane (1994), who found parental education to be an important component of both black-white education differences and the recent trend toward convergence in education levels. Despite the strikingly low levels of education among NELS parents of Mexican heritage, however, the results from Tables 4.2 and 4.3 suggest that maternal education is less important for explaining the graduation gap between whites and Mexican Americans than for explaining the gap between whites and blacks.

The Role of Parental Influences

In this section, we add to the regression models a number of measures that may reflect parents' influence over their children's educational environment. If these measures explain graduation rates and are correlated with parental education or family income, they may help in understanding why parental education and family income have such important effects on educational attainment. Although it is difficult to ascribe causation to the parental influence measures for the reasons provided above, we add these variables to the models in an attempt to shed light on the link between parental education, income, and children's graduation status.

Table 4.4 summarizes our parental influence measures by maternal education and family income to determine the extent to which they are correlated. The first three parental influence measures are an attempt to measure aspects of the literacy environment that the parent seeks to foster in the home. The first measure is a dummy variable equal to 1 if the family usually uses a language other than English.[10] Such families are concentrated toward the low end of the maternal education and family income distributions.

The next measure is a "literacy index" that equals 1 if the family possesses a "literacy bundle" consisting of at least 50 books, an atlas, a daily newspaper, and a regular magazine. The idea is that this measure may reflect a pattern of behavior and consumption indicative of the parents' desire to facilitate literacy and achievement among their children. This measure is strongly correlated with both education and income. High-education families are more than twice as likely to possess the literacy bundle than low-education families; high-income families are more than three times as likely to own it as low-income families.

The next measure equals 1 if the parent reported that the child borrows books from the library on his own behalf. This is a fairly

---

[10]This is a dummy variable equal to 1 if both the student and the parent indicate that the student usually speaks to his parents in a language other than English.

Table 4.4

Indicators of Parental Influence on Students' Education, by Maternal Education and Family Income

Variable	Maternal Education			Family Income		
	Less Than High School	High School Only	Some College or Better	Less Than $10,000	$10,000–$30,000	Greater Than $30,000
Family does not usually use English (%)	8.0	3.0	2.7	5.6	4.3	2.4
Literacy index[a] (%)	20.2	40.6	54.1	16.4	34.4	61.2
Student uses library (%)	66.1	78.2	85.9	68.1	76.8	85.9
Student attends concerts (%)	46.5	59.8	71.9	50.7	59.6	72.5
Family frequently communicates about school matters (student response) (%)	23.6	33.1	44.4	24.0	32.4	45.8
Family frequently communicates about school matters (parent response) (%)	64.3	79.6	85.2	63.6	76.5	86.4
Rules about TV (%)	36.0	36.5	41.1	36.6	37.3	41.0
Rules about homework (%)	41.9	43.6	45.0	43.9	43.8	44.3
Latchkey (%)	29.8	34.7	40.2	33.2	34.8	40.3
Parent belongs to PTO[b] (%)	11.0	28.4	42.6	10.2	23.7	47.3
Parent belongs to other parents' organization (%)	10.3	21.6	34.6	11.1	21.4	35.3
Sample size[c]	1,850	2,732	5,842	1,239	4,977	4,519

NOTE: Based on weighted data.

[a]Equals 1 if family owns a "literacy bundle" consisting of at least 50 books, an atlas, a daily newspaper, and a regular magazine; equals 0 otherwise.

[b]Parent-teacher organization.

[c]Sample sizes add to less than 11,183 because observations with missing values are omitted from these tabulations.

common practice but somewhat more common among higher-education and higher-income families than among others. The next measure equals 1 if the parent indicated that the student attends concerts. We include this measure in part as a check on the library use variable. Both library use and concert attendance are more common among more-advantaged students. Whereas library use may reflect parents' influence in promoting literacy and achievement, it is less obvious that concert attendance would play such a role. Including both measures in the regression may help to determine whether they merely reflect the effects of consumption patterns that are common to high-income families, or whether the potential literacy component of library use exerts an independent effect.

The next two measures are indicators of the extent of communication within the family regarding school-related matters. One item is from the student survey and the other is from the parent survey. The items are not identical, but they are similar enough that it seems instructive to compare them. The student measure equals 1 if the student indicated that he or she frequently discussed with parents both school activities and things studied in class. According to this measure, high-education and high-income families spend more time discussing school-related matters. The parent measure, which equals 1 if the parent indicated frequent discussions with his or her child about school experiences, is also positively correlated with education and income.

The next row shows that the prevalence of rules regarding television is positively correlated with socioeconomic status but that the correlation is fairly weak. Rules about homework are essentially independent of the mother's education and the family's income. The latchkey measure in the next row equals 1 if the student indicated that there is usually no one else at home when the student arrives there after school. Students in high-education and high-income homes are more likely to fall into this category than others. This may be the result of higher employment rates among more-educated mothers.

The last two measures may provide indicators of the social capital of students' families. Membership in PTOs, as well as other organizations involving parents from their children's school, is highly correlated with both maternal education and family income.

Since many of the parental influence measures are highly correlated with maternal education and family income, they potentially could help explain why parental education and income are so important for explaining their children's graduation rates. Of course, to explain the parental education and income effects, they would have to be significant in the high school graduation regressions. If they are significant predictors of graduation rates and are distributed differentially by race/ethnicity, then they could also potentially aid in explaining minority-white graduation gaps.

Table 4.5 presents tabulations of the parental influence measures by race/ethnicity. The first measure indicates, not surprisingly, that almost all of the whites and blacks in the sample speak English with their mothers. In contrast, 24 percent of the Mexican Americans usually speak a foreign language (presumably Spanish) with their families. If the use of English in the home provides important educational advantages for children in American schools, then Mexican Americans are at a substantial disadvantage.

Whites fare better on the literacy index than either blacks or Mexican Americans. Likewise, both library use and concert attendance are somewhat more common among whites than among minority students. The student-based measure of communication regarding school matters is similar among blacks and Mexican Americans but a bit higher among whites. The parent-based measure is highest among whites and lowest among Mexican American families, with blacks falling in between.

Table 4.5

Indicators of Parental Influence on Students' Education, by Race/Ethnicity

Variable	White (1)	Black (2)	Mexican American (3)
Family does not usually use English (%)	1.3	1.0	23.5
Literacy index[a] (%)	48.8	21.1	19.4
Student uses library (%)	81.3	73.7	70.5
Student attends concerts (%)	66.2	63.8	46.1
Family frequently communicates about school matters (student response) (%)	38.9	26.6	30.0
Family frequently communicates about school matters (parent response) (%)	82.0	72.1	65.4
Rules about TV (%)	37.7	44.5	44.8
Rules about homework (%)	44.1	48.6	47.5
Latchkey (%)	39.2	40.3	28.1
Parent belongs to PTO (%)	34.3	29.0	14.4
Parent belongs to other parents' organization (%)	29.5	13.6	14.6

[a]Equals 1 for families that possess the "literacy bundle" consisting of at least 50 books, an atlas, a daily newspaper, and a regular magazine; equals 0 otherwise.

The next row shows that more minority than white students are subject to rules regarding television. If TV viewing is a substitute for doing homework, say, then minority students could benefit from stricter supervision of their TV watching. If rules regarding TV are a response to previous poor performance, however, then the interpretation of this measure becomes more complicated. The next row of the table shows that roughly equal proportions of white, black, and Mexican American students are subject to rules regarding their homework.

About 40 percent of white and black students rate as latchkey children, compared to only 28 percent of Mexican American students. This is a dimension of parental behavior on which Mexican American students appear to be advantaged compared to their white and black counterparts. As for the social capital measures, about 34 percent of white parents belong to their school PTO, which is a somewhat higher rate than the 29 percent of black parents. Both are considerably higher than the 14 percent of Mexican American families. Nearly 30 percent of white parents belong to some other sort of parent organization, compared to only 14 to 15 percent of minority families.

Given their distribution by race/ethnicity, many of these parental influence measures could be capable of explaining minority-white graduation differentials, at least if they predict graduation rates. Table 4.6 reports the results from regressions that include the original family characteristics that appear in Table 4.2 as well as the parental influence measures just discussed. The coefficients on the language use variable appear in the first row of the table. The very few whites who speak a language other than English with their families are significantly more likely to graduate than their counterparts. This could be the result of collinearity between the language use variable and the parental nativity variables, whose coefficients are (algebraically) larger in Table 4.6 than in Table 4.2. Among blacks, the language use measure is insignificant. It is insignificant for the Mexican American students as well. Among U.S.-born and near-native students, speaking Spanish at home appears to confer no particular disadvantage on Mexican Americans.

The literacy index has a positive coefficient in both the white and black subsamples but is significant only for whites. In the Mexican American subsample, it is actually negative though insignificant. Thus

Table 4.6

High School Graduation Regressions Including Indicators of Parental Influence on Students' Education

	White (1)	Black (2)	Mexican American (3)
Family does not usually use English	0.087	−0.076	0.027
	(0.036)	(0.131)	(0.042)
Literacy index	0.031	0.048	−0.016
	(0.011)	(0.048)	(0.049)
Student uses library	0.067	0.079	0.044
	(0.014)	(0.045)	(0.034)
Student attends concerts	0.003	0.009	0.034
	(0.011)	(0.045)	(0.037)
Family frequently communicates about	0.055	0.036	0.099
school matters (student response)	(0.010)	(0.035)	(0.030)
Family frequently communicates about	−0.004	0.062	0.025
school matters (parent response)	(0.014)	(0.048)	(0.039)
Rules about TV	−0.007	0.027	0.011
	(0.012)	(0.036)	(0.030)
Rules about homework	−0.003	−0.058	0.052
	(0.012)	(0.038)	(0.039)
Latchkey	0.000	−0.150	−0.103
	(0.011)	(0.036)	(0.040)
Parent belongs to PTO	0.043	0.029	0.092
	(0.013)	(0.047)	(0.038)
Parent belongs to other parents'	0.022	0.063	0.018
organization	(0.015)	(0.036)	(0.041)
Near-native	−0.026	0.040	0.024
	(0.036)	(0.182)	(0.057)
Female	0.011	0.053	−0.001
	(0.012)	(0.040)	(0.035)
Number of siblings	−0.012	−0.006	−0.029
	(0.004)	(0.011)	(0.012)
Father absent	−0.071	−0.121	−0.066
	(0.020)	(0.047)	(0.048)
Mother born in United States	0.025	−0.058	−0.023
	(0.034)	(0.092)	(0.060)
Father born in United States	−0.033	−0.005	−0.084
	(0.025)	(0.109)	(0.061)
Mother's education			
Less than high school	−0.148	−0.092	0.008
	(0.023)	(0.052)	(0.065)

Table 4.6 (continued)

	White (1)	Black (2)	Mexican American (3)
Some college	−0.001	−0.027	0.048
	(0.013)	(0.039)	(0.059)
College degree	0.023	−0.044	0.007
	(0.014)	(0.096)	(0.068)
Family income			
<$10,000	−0.184	−0.068	−0.299
	(0.034)	(0.070)	(0.059)
$10,000–$15,000	−0.093	−0.026	−0.229
	(0.030)	(0.071)	(0.061)
$15,000–$20,000	−0.038	−0.039	−0.157
	(0.025)	(0.095)	(0.068)
$20,000–$25,000	−0.016	−0.085	−0.124
	(0.020)	(0.073)	(0.061)
$25,000–$30,000	0.005	−0.039	−0.098
	(0.015)	(0.076)	(0.056)
Sample size	8,765	1,325	1,093
Adjusted R-squared	0.150	0.157	0.165

NOTE: Based on weighted data. Figures in parentheses are standard errors that have been adjusted for the presence of multiple students/school and arbitrary forms of heteroskedasticity. In addition to the variables shown, these regressions include the missing value flags described in the notes to Table 4.2.

Mexican American students are unlikely to be educationally disadvantaged by virtue of their families' low scores on this measure.

The library use coefficients are positive and fairly sizable for all three groups and at least marginally significant for whites and blacks. In contrast, the concert attendance measure is quite small for both whites and blacks and insignificant for all three groups. This lends some weight to the notion that it is the literacy-enhancing aspects of library use that affect attainment, rather than merely consumption patterns characteristic of higher-income families.

The student-based communication measure has a positive coefficient for all three groups; for whites and Mexican American students, the coefficients are significant. In contrast, the parent-based communication coefficients are all insignificant and, with the exception of the black coefficient, they are small in magnitude. These results suggest generally that communication between parents and students—as viewed by the student—is an important factor in student attainment. Neither rules about television viewing nor rules about homework have significant effects on graduation rates.

The latchkey coefficients vary considerably by race and ethnicity. Coming home to an empty house appears to have no effect whatsoever on white students. For both black and Mexican American students, however, the latchkey coefficient is negative, sizable, and significant. This difference could be a function of the differences between the neighborhoods in which the different racial/ethnic groups tend to reside. The school fixed-effects analysis below sheds some further light on this issue.

All of the social capital coefficients are positive and at least one of the two coefficients is at least marginally significant in each group. Belonging to a PTO seems important for whites and Mexican American students, whereas other organizations are more important for blacks. Such social ties, which are more common among higher-education and higher-income families, are clearly associated with higher graduation rates.

As a whole, this analysis sheds at least some light on the types of parental influences that are associated with higher attainment on the part of their children. Literacy promotion, as measured by the possession of the literacy bundle and the student's use of the library, is associated with higher graduation rates, although primarily for whites and to some extent for blacks. So too are social capital and frequent communication between the student and parents. Rules about homework and television, in contrast, appear to have little effect. Since many of the influences that appear favorable for the child's graduation prospects are positively correlated with maternal education and family income, it is conceivable that these influences could help explain the maternal education and family income effects that appear in Table 2.4.

To address this issue, we compare the maternal education coefficients from Table 4.6 with the corresponding coefficients in Table 4.2. For whites, adding the parental influence measures reduces the less-than-high-school coefficient a bit. However, it reduces the college degree coefficient by over 60 percent, leaving it insignificant. For blacks, the less-than-high-school coefficient falls, but the other coefficients actually rise. For Mexican American students, adding the parental influence measures has little practical effect, since all of the maternal education coefficients are insignificant in both cases. In summary, there is little evidence that the measures of parental influence explain the maternal education effect for either blacks or Mexican American students. Their explanatory effect for whites is somewhat greater. However, even this finding should be taken as suggestive rather than definitive, since the significance levels of most of the education coefficients are low.

Comparing the family income coefficients from Tables 4.2 and 4.6, we see that adding the parental influence measures to the white regression reduces the coefficients on the lowest two income categories by about 3 percentage points. The next two coefficients fall by about 2 percentage points. Relative to the coefficients in Table 4.2, these amount to reductions of 15 to 60 percent.

For blacks, adding the parental influence variables causes the income coefficients to fall by a fair amount. All of the coefficients fall by about 40 to 60 percent. These changes should be interpreted with caution, however, since the coefficients in Table 4.2 are insignificant.

In the Mexican American regression, all but one of the income coefficients fall by 3 to 5 percentage points when the parental influence measures are added to the model. This amounts to relative reductions of 10 to 30 percent. Thus for all racial/ethnic groups, the parental influence measures appear to offer a partial explanation for the effect of family income on the student's likelihood of graduating.

Table 4.7 provides Oaxaca decompositions of the white-minority graduation gaps based on the regressions in Table 4.6. Consider first the decompositions of the white-black gap that appear in columns (1) and (2). In both cases, mean differences in parental influences help to explain the gap. In the decomposition based on the white coefficients, they explain 2.7 percentage points, or 22 percent of the gap; in the decomposition based on the black coefficients, they explain 4.4 percentage points, or 35 percent. Adding the parental influence variables decreases contribution of the other factors in the model, particularly family income. In both decompositions, differences in mean characteristics now explain essentially the entire white-black graduation gap.

Table 4.7

Oaxaca Decomposition of High School Graduation Differentials from Regressions that Control for Parental Influences

	White-Black		White-Mexican American	
	Based on White Coefficients (1)	Based on Black Coefficients (2)	Based on White Coefficients (3)	Based on Mexican American Coefficients (4)
Percentage of Graduation Differential Attributable to Mean Characteristics				
(1) Family background	3.3	4.1	1.3	−1.3
(2) Mother's education	1.7	1.8	5.8	0.4
(3) Family income	4.6	1.7	4.0	7.7
(4) Parental influence	2.7	4.4	1.4	2.1
(5) Subtotal	12.3	12.0	12.5	8.9
Percentage of Graduation Differential Attributable to Coefficients				
(6) Subtotal	0.2	0.5	−0.3	3.4
Total graduation differential	12.5	12.5	12.2	12.2

NOTE: Based on regression estimates reported in Table 4.6.

For the white-Mexican graduation gap, adding the parental influence measures increases the fraction of the gap explained by mean differences in characteristics, although to a lesser extent. In the decomposition based on the white coefficients, differences in parental influences explain 1.4 percentage points, or 11 percent, of the gap. In the decomposition based on the Mexican American coefficients, they explain 2.1 percentage points, or 17 percent of the gap.

Thus, in addition to shedding at least some light on the parental education and income effects, our parental influence measures help explain part of the white-minority graduation gaps. However, they explain more of the gap for blacks than for Mexican American students. This difference is explained in part by the latchkey measure. Similar numbers of white and black students fend for themselves after school, which means that the latchkey variable explains little of their graduation gap. Because Mexican American students are less likely than whites to be counted as latchkey kids, however, the latchkey variable actually works *against* explaining the white-Mexican graduation gap.

The Role of Schools

Beyond parental behavior, schools have an important influence on graduation rates and may also explain part of the graduation gap between whites and minorities. However, one difficulty in ascertaining the precise role of schools is that readily measured components of school quality, such as teacher training, class sizes, and spending levels, have little effect on students' attainment (Betts, 1996). Moreover, many of these observable school characteristics vary little among the schools attended by white and minority students (Grogger, 1996).

Therefore, to control for the role of schools, we adopt what can be considered a nonparametric approach to characterizing school quality. We include in the regression models school fixed effects, that is, dummy variables for each school. This controls for all differences among schools, both observable and unobservable, that could influence graduation rates. The limitation of this approach is that it does not allow us to assess directly how schools affect graduation rates. However, it does allow us to ask whether differences among schools help to explain the effects of parental education and family income. Indeed, in a system of neighborhood schools, where the school one attends is greatly influenced by the neighborhood in which one lives, and where the value of good schools capitalizes into housing values (Black, 1999), family income might be closely tied to school quality. Given differences in family income by race/ethnicity, schools could play a role in explaining white-minority graduation gaps.

Table 4.8 presents estimates from high school graduation regressions that include school fixed effects. With a few noteworthy exceptions, the estimates in Table 4.8 are largely similar to their counterparts in Table 4.6. The latchkey coefficients for blacks and Mexican American students are about one-third smaller than their counterparts in Table 4.6. In a system of neighborhood schools, school effects are similar to neighborhood effects. This lends credibility to the notion that the magnitude of the latchkey coefficients among minorities, and the difference in the latchkey coefficients between minorities and whites, may have to do with the neighborhoods in which the different racial/ethnic groups tend to reside.

Table 4.8

High School Graduation Regressions with School Fixed Effects

	White (1)	Black (2)	Mexican American
Family does not usually use English	0.064	−0.103	0.026
	(0.037)	(0.149)	(0.041)
Literacy index	0.021	−0.018	−0.022
	(0.009)	(0.043)	(0.056)
Student uses library	0.064	0.062	0.064
	(0.013)	(0.039)	(0.044)
Student attends concerts	0.005	0.026	0.037
	(0.010)	(0.037)	(0.040)
Family frequently communicates about	0.058	0.047	0.094
school matters (student response)	(0.008)	(0.035)	(0.040)
Family frequently communicates about	0.005	0.052	0.017
school matters (parent response)	(0.012)	(0.038)	(0.040)
Rules about TV	−0.009	−0.028	−0.027
	(0.009)	(0.031)	(0.035)
Rules about homework	0.005	−0.006	0.042
	(0.009)	(0.033)	(0.041)
Latchkey	−0.001	−0.100	−0.061
	(0.009)	(0.034)	(0.045)
Parent belongs to PTO	0.044	0.021	0.047
	(0.010)	(0.037)	(0.047)
Parent belongs to other parents'	0.021	0.013	−0.044
organization	(0.009)	(0.047)	(0.056)
Near-native	−0.024	−0.573	0.027
	(0.043)	(0.245)	(0.067)
Female	0.006	−0.011	0.027
	(0.009)	(0.034)	(0.037)
Number of siblings	−0.013	−0.023	−0.024
	(0.004)	(0.010)	(0.012)
Father absent	−0.042	−0.058	−0.046
	(0.012)	(0.039)	(0.047)
Mother born in United States	0.002	−0.150	0.002
	(0.030)	(0.228)	(0.064)
Father born in United States	−0.026	−0.104	−0.065
	(0.027)	(0.133)	(0.061)
Mother's education			
Less than high school	−0.116	−0.064	0.019
	(0.019)	(0.054)	(0.055)
Some college	0.012	−0.017	0.038
	(0.012)	(0.040)	(0.052)
College degree	0.014	0.031	0.043
	(0.014)	(0.058)	(0.100)
Family income			
<$10,000	−0.174	−0.090	−0.255
	(0.026)	(0.061)	(0.071)

Table 4.8 (continued)

	White (1)	Black (2)	Mexican American
$10,000–$15,000	−0.095	−0.055	−0.174
	(0.023)	(0.061)	(0.068)
$15,000–$20,000	−0.046	−0.038	−0.162
	(0.021)	(0.069)	(0.071)
$20,000–$25,000	−0.031	−0.042	−0.079
	(0.017)	(0.065)	(0.061)
$25,000–$30,000	−0.011	0.040	−0.069
	(0.013)	(0.050)	(0.052)
Sample size	8,765	1,325	1,093

NOTE: Based on weighted data. Figures in parentheses are standard errors that have been adjusted for the presence of multiple students/school and arbitrary forms of heteroskedasticity. In addition to the variables shown, these regressions include school dummies and the missing value flags described in the notes to Table 4.2.

Two coefficients that are rendered insignificant by the inclusion of the school dummies are the PTO coefficient in the Mexican American regression and the father-absent coefficient in the black regression. The change in the PTO coefficient suggests that, among Mexican American families, PTO membership is concentrated by schools, making the PTO membership effect difficult to distinguish from a general school effect. The change in the father-absent coefficient is roughly consistent with findings that educational attainment is influenced not only by the student's family structure but also by the fraction of students in his school who live in fatherless families (Grogger, 1997). It suggests that among blacks, single-parent families tend to be concentrated by schools.[11]

---

[11]The near-native coefficient of -0.573 in the black regression is the result of a small numbers problem that arises in the presence of the school fixed effects. There are 14 black near-natives in the sample, each of whom attends a different school. Only eight of the schools contribute to the near-native coefficient, however, since six of the schools have no other black students. In four of the eight schools, the native and near-native graduation rates are the same. In the four schools where the graduation rates differ, the graduation rate differentials between the near-natives and the natives are −1, −0.8, 0.25, and 0.22. Moreover, in the schools with negative differentials, the weight associated with the near-native student exceeded the mean weight associated with the U.S.-born students by a factor of four, on average. In contrast, in the schools with positive differentials, the weights associated with the near-native students averaged only about two-thirds of the

Of course, our main interest focuses on the parental education and income coefficients and specifically on how they change as a result of adding the school dummies to the models. In the white regression, the less-than-high-school coefficient in Table 4.8 is about 3 percentage points smaller than its counterpart in Table 4.6, whereas the other two coefficients are little changed. In the black regressions, adding the school effects reduces the magnitudes of the less-than-high-school and some-college coefficients and turns the college-degree coefficient positive. The college-degree coefficient in the Mexican American regression rises a bit, too. Although caution must be exercised in interpreting these changes, they are consistent with the notion that part of the link between parental education and children's attainment has to do with the schools that the children attend.

As for the family income effect, adding the school dummies to the models has little effect on the coefficients in the white and black regressions. However, it reduces the coefficients in the Mexican American regression by 3 to 4 percentage points, with only one exception. In relative terms, adding the school dummies causes the family income coefficients to fall by 15 to 35 percent. Although these changes are unlikely to be significant, they are consistent with the notion that the strong effects of family income on the graduation prospects of Mexican American students has to do in part with the schools that those students attend.

Unfortunately, in the school fixed effects framework, it is impossible to carry out a full Oaxaca decomposition that would allow one to assess the role of schools in explaining the white-minority graduation gaps. The reason is that the sample includes some schools that are not attended by blacks or Mexican American students and some schools that are not attended by whites. Thus, there is no complete set of regression coefficients that can be used to value the mix of schools attended by the different racial/ethnic groups.

It is possible to carry out a partial decomposition, however. For the partial decomposition, all variables except the school dummies are

---

mean weight associated with the U.S.-born students, hence the large, negative coefficient. Because this coefficient is based on so few observations, its apparent significance should probably be ignored.

decomposed in the usual way. However, the school effects are not decomposed but expressed as a combination of effects attributable to both differences in characteristics (i.e., attendance patterns) and differences in coefficients. Since the school dummies absorb the intercept, it is important to note that the portion of the gap attributable to differences in coefficients has a different interpretation under this partial decomposition than under the complete decompositions above.

Table 4.9 presents the partial decomposition based on the regressions that include the school fixed effects. Since the portion of the gap explained by differences in mean characteristics refers to differences in characteristics net of the effects of schools, the portion of the gap explained by such differences, reported in row (5), is smaller here than in Table 4.7. Adding the school dummies reduces the portion of the white-black graduation gap that is explained by differences in family background and parental influences. The school dummies also reduce

Table 4.9

Decomposition of High School Graduation Differentials from
Regressions That Control for Parental Influences
and School Fixed Effects

	White-Black		White-Mexican American	
	Based on White Coefficients	Based on Black Coefficients	Based on White Coefficients	Based on Mexican American Coefficients
	(1)	(2)	(3)	(4)
Percentage of Graduation Differential Attributable to Mean Characteristics				
(1) Family background	2.3	3.2	0.7	−0.1
(2) Mother's education	1.5	1.4	4.7	0.7
(3) Family income	4.4	2.6	3.9	6.6
(4) Parental influence	2.5	1.7	1.8	1.0
(5) Subtotal	10.7	8.9	11.1	8.2
Percentage of Graduation Differential Attributable to Coefficients				
(6) Subtotal	26.3	28.3	2.6	6.1
Percentage of Graduation Differential Attributable to School Effects (Means and Coefficients)				
(7) Subtotal	−24.7	−24.7	−2.0	−2.0
Total graduation differential	12.5	12.5	12.2	12.2

NOTE: Based on regression estimates reported in Table 4.8.

the effect of differences in family income and parental influences in explaining the white-Mexican gap, particularly in column (4), where the Mexican American coefficients are used to weight the differences in characteristics.

Conclusions

The goals of this chapter were to understand why Mexican Americans receive so little schooling in comparison to both whites and blacks. The data analysis in Appendix B shows that immigration plays a tremendous role in the white-Mexican graduation gap, even among young cohorts of workers. Youths who immigrate to the United States between the ages of 15 and 21 have high school completion rates of only 28 percent, in contrast to the 87 percent completion rate of U.S.-born whites and the 78 percent completion rate of U.S.-born blacks. Mexican youths who arrive in the United States between the ages of 5 and 15 do only a bit better, completing high school at a rate of 40 percent.

Children who arrive before age 5 do much better; about 78 percent complete high school. Indeed their graduation rates are similar to those of both U.S.-born Mexican Americans and blacks. Within their age cohort, U.S.-born and near-native Mexican Americans compose about 65 percent of all persons of Mexican heritage in the United States. We analyze a number of factors to understand why this group graduates at lower rates than whites.

Consistent with prior findings on minority-white attainment differentials, we find that family income plays an important role, explaining as much as 75 percent of the white-Mexican graduation gap. Maternal education, in contrast, plays a very small role, despite the fact that the parents of Mexican American students have very low education levels. The reason is that, for this group, maternal education has little independent effect on students' graduation prospects. This finding helps resolve the heretofore puzzling observation that the educational progress of Mexican Americans seems to stall between the second and third generations. If the intergenerational transmission of educational attainment were as strong among Mexican Americans as among other racial/ethnic groups, then the growth in education between first- and second-generation immigrants would lead to further growth among the third generation. Because the intergenerational transmission mechanism is so much weaker among Mexican Americans, the difference in education between immigrants and their children does not translate into further education gains among subsequent generations. These results are in contrast to those for blacks, for whom maternal education strongly predicts graduation and explains an important fraction of the black-white graduation gap.

In an attempt to illuminate the link between family income and the student's graduation status, we add a number of variables to the model that may reflect the results of parents' actions to influence the educational environment facing their children. Familial communication, social capital, and after-school care arrangements prove helpful both in predicting graduation and in explaining the family income effect for Mexican Americans. Some literacy-related measures such as library use and the possession of reading and reference materials are less important for Mexican American students than they are for whites and blacks, however. The use of Spanish in the home has little effect on graduation one way or the other. There is some evidence that part of the family income effect for Mexican American families operates through the schools that their children attend.

In general, our results confirm the findings of previous studies that point to the importance of family background for explaining graduation rates and graduation rate differentials. We make some headway in understanding at least some of the factors that underlie the link between parental education, family income, and children's educational success. The results leave many further questions, however, such as why certain family characteristics matter more for some racial/ethnic groups than for others, and the role of reverse causation in understanding the insignificance of rules about homework or television viewing. Although it is fairly clear that family characteristics bear importantly on children's educational success, more work is needed to better understand why.

5. Conclusions and Implications for Policy

In this report, we have explored the patterns and determinants of educational attainment and earnings for Mexican Americans in California and the United States. We have sought to understand why Mexican Americans acquire less schooling and earn lower wages than almost any other group in America. We now summarize our findings and discuss the potential implications for public policy.

Education and Wage Patterns

In Chapters 2 and 3, we used recent CPS data to compare the educational attainment and hourly earnings of whites, blacks, and three generations of Mexican Americans (with the first generation consisting of Mexican immigrants, the second generation including the U.S.-born children of Mexican immigrants, and the third generation referring to their grandchildren and later descendants). The main empirical findings of this analysis are as follows:

1. Mexican Americans experience dramatic gains in education and earnings between the first and second generations. On average, U.S.-born Mexican Americans have three and a half years more schooling and at least 30 percent higher wages than do Mexican immigrants.

2. Intergenerational progress for Mexican Americans appears to stall after the second generation, with only modest improvement in educational attainment and no wage growth observed between the second and third generations. A possible reason is that the intergenerational transmission of education is much weaker among Mexican Americans than among other groups. Therefore, the big increase in education that takes place between

immigrants and their children does not translate into further gains among subsequent generations.

3. Substantial education and wage deficits persist between U.S.-born Mexican Americans and other Americans. Among the third generation, for example, Mexican Americans average a year and a half less schooling and about 25 percent lower wages than non-Hispanic whites.

4. The educational disadvantage of Mexican-origin workers is the principal reason why they earn less than other U.S. workers. Among men and women born in the United States, racial/ethnic differences in age and years of schooling explain from one-half to three-quarters of the wage gaps between Mexican American and white workers, with schooling accounting for most of the difference. Thus, to a large extent, Mexican Americans earn low wages because they possess less human capital than other workers. By contrast, observable skill differences account for only about one-third of black-white wage gaps. The contrast between Mexican Americans and blacks in the underlying sources of wage disadvantage is even sharper in California than elsewhere.

5. The labor market payoff to acquiring a high school diploma through an equivalency exam such as the GED, rather than through the usual coursework, is substantially higher for Mexican immigrants than for U.S.-born workers of any racial/ethnic background.

An important implication of these results is that Mexican immigrants and U.S.-born Mexican Americans are distinct groups with very different skills and labor market opportunities, and therefore analyses that do not distinguish between these groups can give a misleading impression of Mexican American economic progress. Though an obvious point and not a new one (see Chavez, 1991), it bears repeating because many media and policy discussions of Mexican Americans continue to lump together immigrants and U.S. natives. Given the strikingly low education and wages of Mexican immigrants, aggregation masks the substantial intergenerational gains that occur. The experiences of second- and third-generation Mexican Americans reveal the long-term economic prospects of the Mexican-origin population, and these prospects are considerably brighter than what is suggested by statistics that do not distinguish between foreign-born and U.S.-born Mexican Americans.

These results also indicate that increasing educational attainment is the key to improving the economic status of Mexican Americans. That more and better schooling would help any group has the ring of a truism, especially in these times of rising demand for skilled workers. But educational improvements are crucial to the earnings progress of Mexican Americans to a much larger extent than for blacks and other disadvantaged groups, because their schooling levels lag behind those of almost all other groups in America. Moreover, the economic payoff to educational investments is about as high for U.S.-born Mexican Americans as for other U.S. natives, especially in California. Finding a way to somehow eliminate the educational disadvantage of Mexican Americans would go a long way toward bringing this group into the economic mainstream. For Mexican immigrants who arrive as teenagers or adults, the GED is a promising avenue for increasing education and ultimate earnings. The GED seems to provide a mechanism through which immigrants can certify their educational qualifications for U.S. employers who do not know how to evaluate credentials earned in Mexico or other foreign countries.

Determinants of High School Graduation

In Chapter 4, we probed the reasons for low graduation rates among Mexican-origin students by using NELS data to investigate the determinants of racial/ethnic differences in high school graduation rates. The first component of this analysis underscored the findings from Chapter 2. Even among young cohorts of workers, the low educational attainment of recent immigrants greatly widens the graduation gap between Mexican Americans and whites. Twenty-four-year-olds who arrived in the United States between the ages of 15 and 21 have high school completion rates of only 28 percent. If these youths have completed all the education that they plan to acquire, closing the graduation gap by increasing the educational attainment of this group seems largely beyond the reach of the traditional U.S. education system.

Education policy conceivably could improve the graduation rate of school-age immigrants, however. School-age immigrants complete high school at a rate of only 40 percent, which is far below the performance of their U.S.-born counterparts. Children who immigrate before age 5 graduate at about the same rate as Mexican Americans. With completion rates of 78 percent, however, these groups still have a graduation gap comparable to that of blacks.

Among U.S.-born and near-native Mexican Americans, we find that family income is an important determinant of the graduation gap. Maternal education is not, however, even though it is an important determinant of educational success for blacks and whites. The weak link between parental education and high school graduation helps explain why, for Mexican American students, intergenerational educational progress appears to stall after the second generation.

Some of the parental influence measures that we analyzed exhibited similar differences by race/ethnicity. Library use and the presence of reading materials in the home help explain graduation rates and the family income effect for whites and blacks, but not for Mexican Americans. Among Mexican Americans, communication in the family, social capital, and after-school care do help explain graduation rates.

On the whole, our analysis makes some progress in understanding the Mexican graduation gap. It also adds to our understanding of why family income is important for explaining graduation rates. Many puzzles remain, however, and there is still much to be learned.

Appendix A

Supplementary Tables

This appendix provides sample sizes and standard errors for some of the estimates from the 1996–1999 CPS data reported in Chapters 2 and 3. Table A.1 displays sample sizes—by gender, race/ethnicity, generation, and location—for the data that underlie the analyses of education and employment in Tables 2.3 to 3.1. Table A.2 gives the same information for the data used in the wage analyses in Tables 3.2 to 3.23. Tables A.3 to A.15 report standard errors for the estimated coefficients in Tables 3.2 to 3.10 and 3.12 to 3.15.

Table A.1

Sample Sizes for CPS Education and Employment Analyses
in Tables 2.3 to 3.1, Ages 25–59

Race/Ethnicity/Generation	U.S. Total	California	Texas	United States Excluding California and Texas
	Men			
Mexican Americans				
Recent immigrant	3,938	1,368	516	2,054
Earlier immigrant	6,537	3,093	1,089	2,355
2nd generation	2,623	895	718	1,010
3rd+ generation	4,866	1,109	1,664	2,093
3rd+ generation whites	237,765	12,578	9,471	215,716
3rd+ generation blacks	25,394	1,580	1,320	22,494
	Women			
Mexican Americans				
Recent immigrant	3,766	1,457	531	1,778
Earlier immigrant	5,494	2,759	1,009	1,726
2nd generation	2,943	1,089	826	1,028
3rd+ generation	5,671	1,294	2,028	2,349
3rd+ generation whites	249,595	13,113	9,890	226,592
3rd+ generation blacks	36,059	1,980	1,901	32,178

SOURCE: 1996–1999 CPS ORG data.

NOTE: Recent immigrants are defined as those who arrived in the United States within approximately 10 years of the survey date.

Table A.2

Sample Sizes for CPS Wage Analyses in Tables 3.2 to 3.23, Wage and Salary Workers, Ages 25–59

Race/Ethnicity/Generation	U.S. Total	California	Texas	United States Excluding California and Texas
Men				
Mexican Americans				
Recent immigrant	3,361	1,153	425	1,783
Earlier immigrant	5,233	2,390	862	1,981
2nd generation	2,067	708	540	819
3rd+ generation	3,794	819	1,340	1,635
3rd+ generation whites	175,615	8,837	7,121	159,657
3rd+ generation blacks	17,880	1,037	982	15,861
Women				
Mexican Americans				
Recent immigrant	1,367	534	173	660
Earlier immigrant	2,677	1,319	472	886
2nd generation	1,851	719	482	650
3rd+ generation	3,658	812	1,313	1,533
3rd+ generation whites	164,130	8,135	6,357	149,638
3rd+ generation blacks	24,082	1,246	1,356	21,480

SOURCE: 1996–1999 CPS ORG data.

NOTE: Recent immigrants are defined as those who arrived in the United States within approximately 10 years of the survey date. The samples for the wage analyses exclude self-employed workers, individuals who work less than 10 hours per week, and those with hourly wages below $1 or above $500.

Table A.3

Standard Errors for Hourly Wage Differentials in Table 3.2, U.S. Total

Race/Ethnicity/Generation	Men			Women		
	(1)	(2)	(3)	(1)	(2)	(3)
Mexican Americans						
Recent immigrant	.008	.008	.008	.013	.013	.012
Earlier immigrant	.007	.007	.007	.009	.009	.009
2nd generation	.010	.010	.009	.011	.011	.010
3rd+ generation	.008	.008	.007	.008	.008	.007
3rd+ generation blacks	.004	.004	.003	.004	.004	.003
Controls for						
Survey month/year	Yes	Yes	Yes	Yes	Yes	Yes
Geographic location	Yes	Yes	Yes	Yes	Yes	Yes
Age	No	Yes	Yes	No	Yes	Yes
Education level	No	No	Yes	No	No	Yes

SOURCE: 1996–1999 CPS ORG data.

NOTE: Recent immigrants are defined as those who arrived in the United States within approximately 10 years of the survey date.

Table A.4

Standard Errors for Hourly Wage Differentials in Table 3.3, California

Race/Ethnicity/Generation	Men			Women		
	(1)	(2)	(3)	(1)	(2)	(3)
Mexican Americans						
Recent immigrant	.017	.017	.019	.024	.025	.026
Earlier immigrant	.013	.012	.015	.016	.016	.018
2nd generation	.021	.020	.019	.021	.021	.019
3rd+ generation	.019	.019	.018	.019	.019	.018
3rd+ generation blacks	.017	.017	.016	.016	.016	.015
Controls for						
Survey month/year	Yes	Yes	Yes	Yes	Yes	Yes
Geographic location	Yes	Yes	Yes	Yes	Yes	Yes
Age	No	Yes	Yes	No	Yes	Yes
Education level	No	No	Yes	No	No	Yes

SOURCE: 1996–1999 CPS ORG data.

NOTE: Recent immigrants are defined as those who arrived in the United States within approximately 10 years of the survey date.

Table A.5

Standard Errors for Hourly Wage Differentials in Table 3.4, Texas

Race/Ethnicity/Generation	Men			Women		
	(1)	(2)	(3)	(1)	(2)	(3)
Mexican Americans						
Recent immigrant	.026	.025	.026	.039	.039	.037
Earlier immigrant	.019	.018	.020	.024	.024	.025
2nd generation	.023	.023	.021	.024	.0224	.022
3rd+ generation	.015	.015	.015	.016	.016	.014
3rd+ generation blacks	.017	.017	.015	.015	.015	.013
Controls for						
Survey month/year	Yes	Yes	Yes	Yes	Yes	Yes
Geographic location	Yes	Yes	Yes	Yes	Yes	Yes
Age	No	Yes	Yes	No	Yes	Yes
Education level	No	No	Yes	No	No	Yes

SOURCE: 1996–1999 CPS ORG data.

NOTE: Recent immigrants are defined as those who arrived in the United States within approximately 10 years of the survey date.

Table A.6

Standard Errors for Hourly Wage Differentials in Table 3.5, United States Excluding California and Texas

Race/Ethnicity/Generation	Men			Women		
	(1)	(2)	(3)	(1)	(2)	(3)
Mexican Americans						
Recent immigrant	.012	.012	.012	.020	.020	.019
Earlier immigrant	.011	.011	.011	.018	.018	.017
2nd generation	.018	.017	.016	.021	.021	.018
3rd+ generation	.013	.013	.012	.014	.014	.013
3rd+ generation blacks	.004	.004	.004	.004	.004	.003
Controls for						
Survey month/year	Yes	Yes	Yes	Yes	Yes	Yes
Geographic location	Yes	Yes	Yes	Yes	Yes	Yes
Age	No	Yes	Yes	No	Yes	Yes
Education level	No	No	Yes	No	No	Yes

SOURCE: 1996–1999 CPS ORG data.

NOTE: Recent immigrants are defined as those who arrived in the United States within approximately 10 years of the survey date.

Table A.7

Standard Errors for Linear Returns to Education in Table 3.6

Race/Ethnicity/Generation	U.S. Total	California	Texas	United States Excluding California and Texas
Men				
Mexican Americans				
Immigrant	.001	.002	.003	.002
2nd generation	.003	.007	.007	.006
3rd+ generation	.003	.008	.005	.005
3rd+ generation whites	.0005	.002	.003	.0005
3rd+ generation blacks	.002	.008	.008	.002
Women				
Mexican Americans				
Immigrant	.002	.003	.005	.003
2nd generation	.004	.008	.007	.007
3rd+ generation	.003	.008	.005	.006
3rd+ generation whites	.0005	.003	.003	.0006
3rd+ generation blacks	.001	.007	.006	.001

SOURCE: 1996–1999 CPS ORG data.

Table A.8

Standard Errors for Nonlinear Returns to Education
in Table 3.7, U.S. Total

Education Level		Mexican Americans		3rd+ Generation Whites	3rd+ Generation Blacks
	Immigrant	2nd Generation	3rd+ Generation		
Men					
8 years or less	.012	.034	.031	.011	.025
Some high school	.014	.028	.021	.005	.011
High school graduate (reference group)					
Some college	.018	.023	.017	.003	.007
Bachelor's degree	.027	.033	.025	.003	.010
Postgraduate degree	.047	.046	.040	.004	.016
Women					
8 years or less	.018	.039	.035	.015	.029
Some high school	.021	.033	.022	.006	.010
High school graduate (reference group)					
Some college	.024	.024	.017	.003	.007
Bachelor's degree	.035	.033	.025	.003	.008
Postgraduate degree	.072	.050	.039	.004	.012

SOURCE: 1996–1999 CPS ORG data.

Table A.9

Standard Errors for Nonlinear Returns to Education in Table 3.8, California

Education Level	Mexican Americans			3rd+ Generation Whites	3rd+ Generation Blacks
	Immigrant	2nd Generation	3rd+ Generation		
Men					
8 years or less	.023	.080	.116	.092	.368
Some high school	.026	.060	.055	.029	.087
High school graduate (reference group)					
Some college	.032	.046	.039	.014	.036
Bachelor's degree	.053	.063	.061	.015	.043
Postgraduate degree	.106	.089	.097	.018	.078
Women					
8 years or less	.031	.085	.117	.111	.337
Some high school	.037	.062	.058	.034	.083
High school graduate (reference group)					
Some college	.041	.044	.039	.014	.036
Bachelor's degree	.065	.062	.061	.015	.043
Postgraduate degree	.156	.105	.080	.019	.058

SOURCE: 1996–1999 CPS ORG data.

Table A.10

Standard Errors for Nonlinear Returns to Education in Table 3.9, Texas

Education Level	Mexican Americans			3rd+ Generation Whites	3rd+ Generation Blacks
	Immigrant	2nd Generation	3rd+ Generation		
Men					
8 years or less	.036	.069	.050	.061	.211
Some high school	.042	.060	.036	.029	.056
High school graduate (reference group)					
Some college	.054	.052	.033	.015	.033
Bachelor's degree	.072	.079	.050	.016	.043
Postgraduate degree	.097	.141	.086	.021	.071
Women					
8 years or less	.050	.073	.054	.073	.135
Some high school	.058	.068	.038	.030	.048
High school graduate (reference group)					
Some college	.070	.054	.031	.015	.028
Bachelor's degree	.086	.074	.045	.016	.037
Postgraduate degree	.149	.099	.091	.022	.055

SOURCE: 1996–1999 CPS ORG data.

Table A.11

Standard Errors for Nonlinear Returns to Education in Table 3.10, United States Excluding California and Texas

Education Level	Mexican Americans			3rd+ Generation Whites	3rd+ Generation Blacks
	Immigrant	2nd Generation	3rd+ Generation		
Men					
8 years or less	.020	.059	.058	.011	.024
Some high school	.023	.051	.038	.005	.011
High school graduate (reference group)					
Some college	.031	.042	.030	.003	.008
Bachelor's degree	.043	.058	.040	.003	.011
Postgraduate degree	.079	.073	.062	.004	.017
Women					
8 years or less	.031	.077	.068	.015	.029
Some high school	.037	.067	.045	.006	.011
High school graduate (reference group)					
Some college	.043	.045	.030	.003	.007
Bachelor's degree	.060	.063	.045	.003	.009
Postgraduate degree	.124	.092	.064	.004	.013

SOURCE: 1996–1999 CPS ORG data.

Table A.12

Standard Errors for Returns to Age in Table 3.12, U.S. Total

Age Group	Mexican Americans			3rd+ Generation Whites	3rd+ Generation Blacks
	Immigrant	2nd Generation	3rd+ Generation		
Men					
25–29 (reference group)					
30–34	.013	.027	.022	.004	.010
35–39	.014	.029	.022	.004	.010
40–44	.016	.031	.022	.004	.011
45–49	.019	.034	.025	.004	.011
50–54	.022	.036	.029	.005	.013
55–59	.027	.037	.036	.005	.015
Women					
25–29 (reference group)					
30–34	.021	.029	.023	.004	.009
35–39	.022	.031	.022	.004	.009
40–44	.023	.033	.024	.004	.009
45–49	.025	.036	.027	.004	.010
50–54	.030	.036	.029	.005	.011
55–59	.036	.041	.037	.005	.013

SOURCE: 1996–1999 CPS ORG data.

Table A.13

Standard Errors for Returns to Age in Table 3.13, California

Age Group	Mexican Americans			3rd+ Generation Whites	3rd+ Generation Blacks
	Immigrant	2nd Generation	3rd+ Generation		
Men					
25–29 (reference group)					
30–34	.024	.052	.055	.019	.049
35–39	.027	.057	.053	.019	.049
40–44	.029	.066	.053	.019	.050
45–49	.035	.080	.060	.020	.053
50–54	.042	.072	.072	.021	.061
55–59	.050	.075	.091	.024	.065
Women					
25–29 (reference group)					
30–34	.036	.054	.058	.019	.049
35–39	.038	.057	.054	.019	.050
40–44	.040	.062	.057	.019	.047
45–49	.044	.067	.068	.019	.052
50–54	.055	.068	.072	.021	.055
55–59	.061	.085	.086	.023	.065

SOURCE: 1996–1999 CPS ORG data.

Table A.14

Standard Errors for Returns to Age in Table 3.14, Texas

Age Group	Mexican Americans			3rd+ Generation Whites	3rd+ Generation Blacks
	Immigrant	2nd Generation	3rd+ Generation		
Men					
25–29 (reference group)					
30–34	.039	.065	.0404	.021	.044
35–39	.041	.064	.040	.020	.045
40–44	.048	.070	.043	.020	.049
45–49	.051	.072	.049	.022	.048
50–54	.057	.079	.052	.023	.059
55–59	.066	.080	.069	.026	.079
Women					
25–29 (reference group)					
30–34	.059	.066	.041	.021	.039
35–39	.062	.069	.041	.021	.037
40–44	.063	.074	.043	.021	.040
45–49	.069	.074	.049	.021	.041
50–54	.074	.075	.050	.023	.051
55–59	.091	.078	.067	.028	.058

SOURCE: 1996–1999 CPS ORG data.

Table A.15

Standard Errors for Returns to Age in Table 3.15, United States Excluding California and Texas

Age Group	Mexican Americans			3rd+ Generation Whites	3rd+ Generation Blacks
	Immigrant	2nd Generation	3rd+ Generation		
Men					
25–29 (reference group)					
30–34	.021	.050	.039	.004	.011
35–39	.023	.052	.039	.004	.011
40–44	.026	.053	.038	.004	.011
45–49	.030	.058	.043	.004	.012
50–54	.036	.066	.053	.005	.013
55–59	.047	.067	.062	.005	.015
Women					
25–29 (reference group)					
30–34	.035	.057	.041	.004	.010
35–39	.038	.058	.040	.004	.010
40–44	.041	.061	.043	.004	.010
45–49	.047	.073	.046	.004	.010
50–54	.052	.073	.055	.005	.012
55–59	.075	.089	.069	.005	.014

SOURCE: 1996–1999 CPS ORG data.

Appendix B

Comparison of NELS and CPS Education Data

In this appendix, we compare the NELS data with data from comparable-age samples from the CPS. This provides us with a means of gauging how representative the NELS is of various subpopulations of U.S. youths.

Column (1) of Table B.1 reports high school completion rates by race and ethnicity for 18- to 24-year-olds from the October 1994 survey. We focus on the 1994 CPS because our graduation data in the NELS were also collected in 1994. Our tabulations of the CPS yield results that are nearly identical to those from official Census Bureau publications.[1]

The next column uses the same CPS sample but a different race/ethnicity classification scheme that is the same as that used in the NELS. In column (2), the race/ethnicity classifications are mutually exclusive, with Hispanic taking priority. Thus, white and black could be referred to more precisely as white non-Hispanic and black non-Hispanic.[2] In the Census classification scheme used in column (1), in contrast, the categories white and black are mutually exclusive, but Hispanics may be of any race, with the result that many Hispanic are double-counted.

These two classification schemes produce the same completion rates for Hispanics (and likewise for the subcategories Mexican American and other Hispanic), but they yield different completion rate differentials. The reason is that the 1,140 Hispanics who also classified themselves as white under the Census race categories had lower completion rates, on average, than non-Hispanic whites, with the result that the white high school completion rate under the mutually exclusive classification scheme

---

[1]See U.S. Bureau of the Census (1996).

[2]This is the classification scheme used in Chapters 2 and 3.

Table B.1

High School Completion Rates in the October 1994 CPS and the NELS

Race/Ethnicity	CPS, 18–24[a] (1)	CPS, 18–24[b] (2)	CPS, 19–21[b] (3)	NELS[b] (4)
White	82.6	87.1	88.5	90.4
	[9,901]	[8,761]	[3,596]	[8,906]
Black	77.3	77.6	77.9	83.4
	[1,492]	[1,469]	[609]	[1,376]
Hispanic	56.5	56.5	62.1	81.2
	[1,395]	[1,395]	[590]	[1,680]
Mexican American	52.7	52.7	57.4	79.2
	[869]	[869]	[366]	[1,183]
Other Hispanic	64.7	64.7	69.8	85.8
	[526]	[526]	[224]	[497]
Sample size	11,625	11,625	4,795	11,962

NOTE: Figures in brackets are cell sizes.

[a]Based on a Census-type race/ethnicity classification by which white and black are mutually exclusive categories but Hispanics may be of any race.

[b]Based on a race/ethnicity classification by which white, black, and Hispanic are mutually exclusive categories where Hispanic takes precedence.

is 87.1 percent, 4.5 percentage points higher than under the Census classification scheme. Thus, the white-Mexican completion rate differential from column (2) is 34.4 percentage points, rather than 29.9 percentage points, as in column (1). This is substantially greater than the 9.5 percentage point gap that exists between blacks and whites under the mutually exclusive classification scheme of column (2).

Also worth noting is the difference in completion rates between Hispanics of Mexican heritage and other Hispanics. Mexican Americans, who account for almost 60 percent of the U.S. Hispanic population in this age group, have a high school completion rate of only 52.7 percent, nearly 25 percentage points lower than that of blacks. Other Hispanics, who include mostly Puerto Ricans, Cubans, and Central Americans, have a completion rate of only 64.7 percent, which is lower than the completion rate of blacks but considerably higher than the completion rate of people of Mexican heritage. Indeed the completion rate differential between the two Hispanic groups is greater than that between whites and blacks.

Column (3) presents completion rates for 19- to 21-year-olds. This age span is closer to that of the NELS sample than is the conventional Census age grouping. The high school completion rates for whites and blacks are essentially the same for the 19- to 21-year-olds as for the 18- to 24-year-olds. For both Hispanic groups, however, completion rates are about 5 percentage points higher for the 19- to 21-year-olds.

Finally, column (4) presents completion rates for the NELS sample. For both whites and blacks, high school completion rates are a bit higher in the NELS than in the CPS. This suggests that the NELS misses some of the most educationally disadvantaged students. For Hispanics, however, the completion rate from the NELS is nearly 20 percentage points higher than that from the CPS, and for persons of Mexican heritage, the differential is nearly 22 percentage points. Clearly, the NELS missed many Mexican Americans without high school credentials who were ages 19–21 in 1994.

Table B.2 shows that much of the differential between the two surveys is attributable to differential coverage of immigrants. Indeed, many of the immigrants who appear in the CPS could never have been captured by the NELS. Column (4) of Table B.2 shows that 23 percent of Mexican Americans in the 19–21 age group arrived in the United States after age 15. These individuals are excluded from our NELS sample by virtue of both the NELS design and our sample inclusion criteria. First, the vast majority of students who were in eighth grade in 1988 were under age 15, so by definition either must have been U.S.-born or must have immigrated before age 15. Second, although the NELS "freshened" its sample in 1990 and 1992 by drawing in new students, we exclude such students because they did not participate in the 1988 survey that provides the family background data crucial for our analysis above. These late immigrants in the CPS have an incredibly low high school completion rate of only 28.2 percent. One main reason for the discrepancy between the NELS and the CPS is the absence of this large group of late immigrants from the NELS.

Table B.2

High School Completion Rates, by Race/Ethnicity and Nativity

Race/Ethnicity	19- to 21-Year-Olds in October 1994 CPS				NELS		
	U.S.-Born	Immigrated Before Age 5	Immigrated Between Ages 5 and 15	Immigrated After Age 15	U.S.-Born	Immigrated Before Age 5	Immigrated Between Ages 5 and 15
	(1)	(2)	(3)	(4)	(5)	(6)	(7)
White	88.6	86.8	86.8	84.4	90.6	90.3	94.5
	[3,499]	[45]	[15]	[37]	[8,670]	[95]	[42]
	(97)	(1)	(0)	(0)	(98)	(1)	(1)
Black	79.1	73.0	72.0	52.1	83.0	83.4	100.0
	[566]	[6]	[17]	[20]	[1,311]	[14]	[22]
	(93)	(1)	(3)	(3)	(97)	(1)	(2)
Mexican American	70.0	77.8	39.9	28.2	79.6	77.9	71.8
	[201]	[35]	[45]	[85]	[978]	[115]	[45]
	(55)	(10)	(12)	(23)	(86)	(10)	(4)
Other Hispanic	75.9	86.9	64.8	55.6	86.2	97.1	71.8
	[99]	[23]	[49]	[53]	[403]	[31]	[41]
	(44)	(10)	(22)	(24)	(85)	(7)	(9)
Sample size[a]	4,365	109	126	197	11,362	255	150

NOTE: Figures in brackets are cell sizes and figures in parentheses are within-sample row percentages, which may not sum to 1 because of rounding.

[a]There were 195 students in the NELS whose nativity could not be determined.

They are not the only reason, however. Students who immigrated between the ages of 5 and 15 could have been sampled by the NELS in eighth grade, at least in principle. Yet column (7) shows that this group constitutes only 4 percent of the Mexican American students in the NELS, whereas column (3) shows that it constitutes 12 percent of the Mexican American cohort in the CPS. Moreover, the school-age immigrants in the NELS do substantially better than their counterparts in the CPS, completing high school at a rate of 71.8 percent rather than 39.9 percent. It may be that the NELS simply missed most school-age immigrants, which is consistent with the observation that the NELS undercovered non-English speakers (National Center for Education Statistics, 1994). Alternatively, given their low graduation rates in the CPS, it may be that most of these children had already left school before the end of eighth grade. Whatever the precise reasons, it is clear that the NELS is of little use for analyzing high school completion patterns among people who immigrate during or after their school-age years.

At the same time, however, high school completion rates for "near-natives"—children who arrive in the United States before age 5—are nearly identical in the NELS and the CPS, at 78 percent. For U.S.-born Mexican Americans, the CPS yields a completion rate of 70 percent, the upper end of whose 95 percent confidence interval, at 76 percent, is close to the NELS-based estimate of 79.6 percent. Taken together, the groups of U.S.-born and near-native Mexican Americans in the NELS appear to be fairly comparable to their counterparts in the CPS. We conclude that although the NELS is not at all representative of immigrants who arrive during their school-age years, it seems reasonably representative of the U.S.-born and near-native population of whites, blacks, and people of Mexican origin. This includes nearly two-thirds of the Mexican American population in this age cohort.

Bibliography

Abowd, John M., and Mark R. Killingsworth, "Do Minority/White Unemployment Differences Really Exist?" *Journal of Business and Economic Statistics*, Vol. 2, No. 1, January 1984, pp. 64–72.

Bean, Frank D., and Marta Tienda, *The Hispanic Population of the United States*, Russell Sage Foundation, New York, 1987.

Bean, Frank D., Stephen J. Trejo, Randy Capps, and Michael Tyler, *The Latino Middle Class: Myth, Reality, and Potential*, Tomas Rivera Policy Institute, Claremont, California, 2001.

Becker, Gary S., *A Treatise on the Family*, Harvard University Press, Cambridge, Massachusetts, 1981.

Betts, Julian R., "Is There a Link Between School Inputs and Earnings? Fresh Scrutiny of an Old Literature," in Gary Burtless, ed., *Does Money Matter? The Effect of School Resources on Student Achievement and Adult Success*, Brookings Institution Press, Washington, D.C., 1996.

Betts, Julian R., *The Changing Role of Education in the California Labor Market*, Public Policy Institute of California, San Francisco, California, 2000.

Black, Sandra E., "Do Better Schools Matter? Parental Valuation of Elementary Education," *Quarterly Journal of Economics*, Vol. 114, No. 2, May 1999, pp. 577–599.

Borjas, George J., "The Economic Status of Male Hispanic Migrants and Natives in the United States," *Research in Labor Economics*, Vol. 6, 1984, pp. 65–122.

Borjas, George J., "Immigrant and Emigrant Earnings: A Longitudinal Study," *Economic Inquiry*, Vol. 27, No. 1, January 1989, pp. 21–37.

Borjas, George J., "The Intergenerational Mobility of Immigrants," *Journal of Labor Economics*, Vol. 11, No. 1, Part 1, January 1993, pp. 113–135.

Borjas, George J., "Immigrant Skills and Ethnic Spillovers," *Journal of Population Economics*, Vol. 7, No. 2, 1994, pp. 99–118.

Borjas, George J., "Assimilation and Changes in Cohort Quality Revisited: What Happened to Immigrant Earnings in the 1980s?" *Journal of Labor Economics*, Vol. 13, No. 2, April 1995, pp. 201–245.

Bratsberg, Bernt, and James F. Ragan, Jr., "The Importance of Host-Country Schooling on Earnings: A Study of Male Immigrants in the United States," *Journal of Human Resources*, Vol. 37, No. 1, Winter 2002, pp. 63–105.

Cameron, Stephen V., and James J. Heckman, "The Nonequivalence of High School Equivalents," *Journal of Labor Economics*, Vol. 11, No. 1, Part 1, January 1993, pp. 1–47.

Cameron, Stephen V., and James J. Heckman, "The Dynamics of Educational Attainment for Blacks, Hispanics, and Whites," *Journal of Political Economy*, Vol. 109, No. 3, June 2001, pp. 455–499.

Chapa, Jorge, "The Myth of Hispanic Progress: Trends in the Educational and Economic Attainment of Mexican Americans," *Journal of Hispanic Policy*, Vol. 4, 1990, pp. 3–18.

Chavez, Linda, *Out of the Barrio: Toward a New Politics of Hispanic Assimilation*, Basic Books, New York, 1991.

Chiswick, Barry R., "The Effect of Americanization on the Earnings of Foreign-Born Men," *Journal of Political Economy*, Vol. 86, No. 5, October 1978, pp. 897–921.

Clark, Melissa A., and David A. Jaeger, "Natives, the Foreign-Born and High School Equivalents: New Evidence on the Returns to the GED," manuscript, Princeton University, Princeton, New Jersey, 2000.

Darity, William, Jr., David Guilkey, and William Winfrey, "Ethnicity, Race, and Earnings," *Economics Letters*, Vol. 47, No. 3/4, March 1995, pp. 401–408.

Grogger, Jeffrey, "Does School Quality Explain the Recent Black White Wage Trend?" *Journal of Labor Economics*, Vol. 14, No. 2, April 1996, pp. 231–253.

Grogger, Jeffrey, "Local Violence and Educational Attainment," *Journal of Human Resources*, Vol. 32, No. 4, Fall 1997, pp. 659–682.

Haveman, Robert, and Barbara Wolfe, *Succeeding Generations: On the Effects of Investments in Children*, Russell Sage Foundation, New York, 1994.

Heckman, James J., "Sample Selection Bias as a Specification Error," *Econometrica*, Vol. 47, No. 1, January 1979, pp. 153–161.

Hu, Wei-Yin, "Assimilation and the Earnings of Immigrants: New Evidence from Longitudinal Data," manuscript, University of California, Los Angeles, California, 1999.

Jasso, Guillermina, and Mark R. Rosenzweig, "How Well Do U.S. Immigrants Do? Vintage Effects, Emigration Selectivity, and Occupational Mobility," *Research in Population Economics*, Vol. 6, 1988, pp. 229–253.

Juhn, Chinhui, Kevin M. Murphy, and Brooks Pierce, "Wage Inequality and the Rise in Returns to Skill," *Journal of Political Economy*, Vol. 101, No. 3, June 1993, pp. 410–442.

Kane, Thomas J., "College Entry by Blacks Since 1970: The Role of College Costs, Family Background, and the Returns to Education," *Journal of Political Economy*, Vol. 102, No. 5, October 1994, pp. 878–911.

Levy, Frank, and Richard J. Murnane, "U.S. Earnings Levels and Earnings Inequality: A Review of Recent Trends and Proposed Explanations," *Journal of Economic Literature*, Vol. 30, No. 3, September 1992, pp. 1333–1381.

Lubotsky, Darren, "Chutes or Ladders? A Longitudinal Analysis of Immigrant Earnings," Working Paper 445, Princeton University Industrial Relations Section, Princeton, New Jersey, 2000.

McKinney, Kevin, "Mexican American High School Dropouts: Why Is There No Intergenerational Progress?" manuscript, University of California, Santa Barbara, California, 1999.

Murnane, Richard J., John B. Willett, and John H. Tyler, "Who Benefits from Obtaining a GED? Evidence from High School and Beyond," *Review of Economics and Statistics*, Vol. 82, No. 1, February 2000, pp. 23–37.

Murphy, Kevin M., and Finis Welch, "The Structure of Wages," *Quarterly Journal of Economics*, Vol. 107, No. 1, February 1992, pp. 285–326.

National Center for Education Statistics, *Second Follow-Up: Student Component Data Files Users Manual*, Washington, D.C., 1994.

Oaxaca, Ronald L., and Michael R. Ransom, "On Discrimination and the Decomposition of Wage Differentials," *Journal of Econometrics*, Vol. 61, No. 1, March 1994, pp. 5–21.

Oaxaca, Ronald L., and Michael R. Ransom, "Identification in Detailed Wage Decompositions," *Review of Economics and Statistics*, Vol. 81, No. 1, February 1999, pp. 154–157.

Reed, Deborah, *California's Rising Income Inequality: Causes and Concerns*, Public Policy Institute of California, San Francisco, California, 1999.

Reed, Deborah, Melissa Glenn Haber, and Laura Mameesh, *The Distribution of Income in California*, Public Policy Institute of California, San Francisco, California, 1996.

Reimers, Cordelia W., "Labor Market Discrimination Against Hispanic and Black Men," *Review of Economics and Statistics,* Vol. 65, No. 4, November 1983, pp. 570–579.

Reimers, Cordelia W., "Sources of the Family Income Differentials Among Hispanics, Blacks, and White Non-Hispanics," *American Journal of Sociology*, Vol. 89, No. 4, January 1984, pp. 889–903.

Reyes, Belinda I., *Dynamics of Immigration: Return Migration to Western Mexico*, Public Policy Institute of California, San Francisco, California, 1997.

Reyes, Belinda I., ed., *A Portrait of Race and Ethnicity in California: An Assessment of Social and Economic Well-Being*, Public Policy Institute of California, San Francisco, California, 2001.

Schoeni, Robert F., "New Evidence on the Economic Progress of Foreign-Born Men in the 1970s and 1980s," *Journal of Human Resources*, Vol. 32, No. 4, Fall 1997, pp. 683–740.

Smith, James P., "Hispanics and the American Dream: An Analysis of Hispanic Male Labor Market Wages 1940–1980," manuscript, RAND, Santa Monica, California, 1991.

Trejo, Stephen J., "Why Do Mexican Americans Earn Low Wages?" *Journal of Political Economy*, Vol. 105, No. 6, December 1997, pp. 1235–1268.

U.S. Bureau of the Census, *School Enrollment—Social and Economic Characteristics of Students: October 1994*, Series P20-487, U.S. Government Printing Office, Washington, D.C., 1996.

Waters, Mary C., *Ethnic Options: Choosing Identities in America*, University of California Press, Berkeley, California, 1990.

About the Authors

JEFFREY GROGGER

Jeffrey Grogger, a professor of public policy at the University of California, Los Angeles, is an economist whose research focuses on problems of the low-income population. He has written widely on welfare reform, the link between youth crime and the labor market, the economic consequences of teen childbearing, and the economics of education. He is a research associate of the National Bureau of Economic Research (Cambridge, Massachusetts) and a research fellow of the Institute for the Study of Labor (Bonn, Germany) and the Center for Economic Policy Research (London). He also serves as co-editor of the *Journal of Human Resources*.

STEPHEN J. TREJO

Stephen Trejo is an associate professor of economics at the University of Texas, Austin. His research focuses on public policy issues involving labor markets, including overtime pay regulation, the experiences of immigrants, and obstacles to the economic progress of minority groups. Much of his recent work analyzes patterns of intergenerational improvement among Mexican Americans. He holds a B.A. from the University of California, Santa Barbara, and a Ph.D. in economics from the University of Chicago.

Other Related PPIC Publications

California in the New Millennium: The Changing Social and Political Landscape
Mark Baldassare

The Changing Role of Education in the California Labor Market
Julian R. Betts

"At Home and in School: Racial and Ethnic Gaps in Educational Preparedness"
California Counts: Population Trends and Profiles
Volume 3, Number 2, November 2001
Jennifer Y. Cheng

California's Rising Income Inequality: Causes and Concerns
Deborah Reed

"Poverty in California: Levels, Trends, and Demographic Dimensions"
California Counts: Population Trends and Profiles
Volume 3, Number 3, November 2001
Deborah Reed, Richard Van Swearingen

A Portrait of Race and Ethnicity in California: An Assessment of Social and Economic Well-Being
Belinda I. Reyes (editor) et al.

"The Linguistic Landscape of California Schools"
California Counts: Population Trends and Profiles
Volume 3, Number 4, February 2002
Sonya M. Tafoya

PPIC publications may be ordered by phone or from our website
(800) 232-5343 [mainland U.S.]
(415) 291-4400 [Canada, Hawaii, overseas]
www.ppic.org